Migration, Remittances and 'Development' in Lesotho

Jonathan Crush, Belinda Dodson, John Gay, Thuso Green and Clement Leduka

Series Editor:
Prof. Jonathan Crush

Southern African Migration Programme
2010

ACKNOWLEDGEMENTS

The research for this paper was conducted by Sechaba Consultants, the Lesotho partner for the Southern African Migration Project (SAMP). The national Lesotho migration and remittances survey (MARS), conducted in 2005, provided the quantitative database for the study. The qualitative interviews and focus groups for this study were conducted in 2008-9 by a team led by David Hall of Sechaba Consultants. We are grateful to him and his researchers as well as the following for their assistance: Wade Pendleton, Abel Chikanda, Bruce Frayne, Krista House, Dave Dorey and Christa Schier. We also wish to thank Ashley Hill, Cassandra Eberhardt, Jennie Payne and Maria Salamone for their editorial help. Finally, thanks are due to DFID-UK for funding the MARS survey, to UN-INSTRAW for funding the qualitative research and to IDRC for its support of the SAMP project on "Migration, Poverty and Development in Southern Africa."

Published by Idasa, 6 Spin Street, Church Square, Cape Town, 8001, and Southern African Research Centre, Queen's University, Canada.

Copyright Southern African Migration Programme (SAMP) 2010
ISBN 978-1-920409-26-5
First published 2010
Design by Bronwen Müller

CONTENTS   PAGE

FIGURES   PAGE

EXECUTIVE SUMMARY

L esotho is one of the most migration dependent countries in the world. Migrant remittances are the country's major source of foreign exchange, accounting for 25% of GDP in 2006. Lesotho is also one of the poorest countries in the world due to high domestic unemployment, declining agricultural production, falling life expectancy, rising child mortality and half the population living below the poverty line. The majority of households and rural communities are dependent on remittances for their livelihood. Households without access to migrant remittances are significantly worse off than those that do have such access.

Since 1990, patterns of migration from Lesotho to South Africa have changed dramatically. These changes include significant increases in legal and irregular cross-border movement between Lesotho and South Africa; declining employment opportunities for Basotho men in the South African gold mines; increased female migration from Lesotho; growing internal female migration of young women within Lesotho; a 'brain drain' from Lesotho to South Africa and the growth of AIDS-related migration in Lesotho. The central question addressed in this report is how these changes have impacted remittance flows and usage.

For most of the twentieth century, the vast majority of migrants from Lesotho were single young men who went to work on the South African gold mines and remitted funds to their parents' households. Migration has become much more mixed in recent years and the profile of migrants leaving Lesotho has changed significantly:

- The number of Basotho male migrants working on the mines declined from 100,000 in 1990 to 46,000 in 2006. However, the majority of male migrants from Lesotho are still mineworkers.
- The demographic profile of male migrants has shifted markedly. Migrants used to be single young men. Now 84% are married and 77% are heads of households. Nearly 50% of migrants are over the age of 40 and only 5% are under 25.
- Half of the growing number of female migrants from Lesotho are domestic workers in South Africa. The rest are spread between the informal sector (9%), commercial farmwork (5%), self-employed businesses (6%), the professions (5%) and skilled manual work (5%). In other words, although one sector dominates, female migrants work in a wider variety of jobs than males.
- On the whole, female migrants are younger than males but significant numbers of older women are also migrants. In contrast to male migrants, only 27% of female migrants are married. On the other hand, 42% are divorced, separated, abandoned or widowed.

Most older women migrants fall into this category. A sizable group of women thus has the responsibility of being the head of their own household but have to migrate to South Africa in order to ensure the survival of the household.

- Over 40,000 young, mostly single, women are "internal migrants" working in Lesotho's textile factories. The textile workers have been called the 'new miners' though wages in the factories are paltry compared with the mines. If the textile industry did not exist, or closed down, then most of these women would probably migrate to South Africa.
- Most migrants who work outside mining are irregular migrants as the South African government is reluctant to give them work permits. This increases their vulnerability to exploitation. Many women are in South Africa on 30-day visitor's passes and are supposed to return to Lesotho every 30 days to renew them. If they do not, they have to pay a "fine" when they eventually return home.

Changes in the profile of migration from Lesotho have impacted on remittance flows in a number of ways:

- The decline in mine employment has not led to a decrease in remittance flows to Lesotho. On the contrary, total remittance flows increased as a result of increases in mine wages. But rising remittance flows are directed to a shrinking number of households thus increasing inequality between households and accelerating levels of poverty and food insecurity for households that do not have a mineworker.
- Female domestic workers in South Africa remit less to Lesotho than male miners. This is primarily because they earn about a third as much as their male counterparts. Domestic workers are notoriously exploited in South Africa.
- Some migrants have second families or partners in South Africa. In the case of male migrants, this tends to reduce the amount remitted to Lesotho. In the case of female migrants, it often increases the flow of remittances as they are able to remit some of their partner's earnings back home as well.
- The vast majority of cash remittances flow through informal channels (usually carried by hand). Only 5% of migrants use the Post Office and 2% the banks to remit.

Remittance-receiving households in Lesotho tend to use most of the remittances for basic needs:

- Migrant remittances form an important, and in many cases, the only, source of income for migrant-sending households in Lesotho. Over 95% of the households with male migrant members and 90% with female migrant members list remittances as a source of household income. Fewer than 10% list income from the second-ranking income source, non-migrant wage labour.

- Most households (89%) say that the contribution of remittances to household income is important or very important. Remittances are also key to having enough food in the household (with nearly 90% saying that it is important or very important).

- The most common use of remittances is for food (90% of households spend remittances on food), clothing (76%), school fees (56%) and fares for transportation (34%).

- Almost three quarters of households do not invest remittances in agriculture. Of those that do, a quarter spend remittances on seed, 18% on fertilizer, 12% on tractors and 4% on livestock. Nearly 19% of households put some remittance income into savings. Other expenditures such as funerals (incurred by 16% of households) and funeral and burial insurance policies (29%) reflect the impact of HIV and AIDS.

- Households with female migrants are more likely to supplement remittance earnings with other sources of income.

- Remittances are not used on luxury consumer items but are used, directly or indirectly, to meet the household's subsistence needs.

- The proportion of households investing remittances in formal or informal business is extremely low.

- In the rural villages, remittances are often "pooled" by women through burial societies, grocery associations and egg circles. As well as loaning money to be paid back with interest, the associations buy food and groceries in bulk to divide up among members.

Remittances are essential to household survival in Lesotho but the opportunities for investing remittances in productive, developmental activities are very limited. This suggests that it is important to stop seeing Lesotho as the only site for entrepreneurship by migrants from there. Companies from all over the world are permitted to come and do business in South Africa. The same opportunity should be afforded to Basotho households. Basotho should also be freely allowed to do business in South Africa. Instead, migrants are more often viewed as a threat and undesirable. Migration needs to be re-thought as something that is mutually beneficial for both countries. The only realistic option is to open the borders for unrestricted travel in both directions and to allow Basotho to pursue economic opportunities in South Africa free of harassment and deportation.

INTRODUCTION

Lesotho is one of the most migration-dependent countries in the world. Out of a population of around two million people, over 240,000 were recently estimated to be outside the country.[1] Migrant remittances are the country's major source of foreign exchange, accounting for 25% of GDP in 2006. Lesotho is also one of the poorest countries in the world due to high domestic unemployment, declining agricultural production, falling life expectancy, rising child mortality and half the population living below the poverty line. The majority of households and rural communities are dependent on remittances for their livelihood. Households without access to migrant remittances are significantly worse off than those that do have such access. According to the 2006 Lesotho National Human Development Report, "Migrant labourers' remittances have played a critical role in providing household incomes over a long period of time. Remittances from Basotho migrant labourers in South Africa have allowed households to reduce their dependence on agriculture and make investments to supplement their farming activities."[2] While it is true that dependence on remittances stretches back many decades, this conclusion is highly misleading. Indeed, it is only possible because of a basic lack of reliable, representative data on remittance flows, uses and impacts at the household level.

The relationship between migration, development and remittances in Lesotho has been exhaustively studied for the period up to 1990.[3] This was an era when the vast majority of migrants from Lesotho were young men working on the South African gold mines and over 50 percent of households had a migrant mineworker. Since 1990, patterns of migration to South Africa have changed dramatically. The reconfiguration of migration between the two countries has had a marked impact on remittance flows to Lesotho. The central question addressed in this report is how the change in patterns of migration from and within Lesotho since 1990 has impacted on remittance flows and usage. Large claims have recently been made by agencies such as the World Bank about the development potential of migrant remittances.[4] In Lesotho, as this report will demonstrate, such claims are overly optimistic. Remittance flows are a highly significant (often the only) source of income for many households. The loss of remittances would plunge them into destitution, a fact that does not suggest they are in a position to escape the "trap" of remittances-dependence through other sustainable forms of income generation.

Unlike in many migrant-sending countries, the contribution of remittances to poverty reduction and to development prospects in Lesotho has been increasingly recognized at the policy level. In Lesotho's 2004 Poverty Reduction Strategy Paper (PRSP), for example, "migration features quite prominently in relation to discussion of the changing nature of livelihood and poverty trends over the last two decades."[5] Lesotho's 2006 National Human Development Report mentions the significance of migration to households on several occasions but misleadingly suggests that it has become less important since 1990.[6] The country's presentation at the 2006 UN High Level Dialogue on International Migration and Development in New York also recognized the importance of development-oriented regional and national migration policies.[7] Lesotho is committed to implementation of the African Union's Strategic Framework on International Migration and Common Position on Migration and Development. Furthermore, Lesotho is the only country in Southern Africa to have ratified the UN International Convention on the Protection of the Rights of All Migrant Workers and Members of their Families. Lesotho is also an active participant in the Migration Dialogue for Southern Africa (MIDSA), an inter-governmental forum for policy dialogue on migration within SADC.[8]

How to harness the potential of migration for development is a major challenge for Lesotho.[9] In order to initiate such a debate (in Lesotho and South Africa), a comprehensive overview of Lesotho's contemporary migration patterns and trends is required. Secondly, there is a need for nationally representative household data on remittance flows and their uses and impacts. Thirdly, data on migration and remittances must be disaggregated by gender in order to assess how changes in female migration are impacting remittance flows. Finally, information is needed on whether remittances are simply used for household basic needs or spent on consumer goods (as is commonly assumed) or whether, in fact, remittances are used for savings, investment and further wealth-generation for the household, community and country.

The data collected for this project and the analysis that follows provide many new insights into the critical role of migration and remittances in contemporary Lesotho. The policy implications of these findings are considerable although, in general, they suggest that enthusiasm for the development potential of remittances requires serious qualification in the case of Lesotho. As this report argues, the dependence on remittances for basic needs means that there is very little surplus for entrepreneurial ventures. And, even if there was, the structural constraints on entrepreneurship are such that it is doubtful this would lead to a new remittance-led form of development in Lesotho. Nonetheless, this report examines the obstacles to the 'full enjoyment' by households and communities of their remittance packages. This basic finding – of the non-developmental role of remittances in contemporary Lesotho – leads in turn to a broader policy conclusion: enterprising Basotho will continue to be frustrated as long as they are denied free access to the South African labour market and the opportunity to try their entrepreneurial skills and instincts not just in Lesotho but in South Africa as well.

METHODOLOGY

SAMP has been systematically studying the relationship between migration, remittances and development in Southern Africa since 2000. Given the paucity of data on the subject, a multi-country research initiative on migration and remittances was launched in Botswana, Lesotho, Malawi, Mozambique, Swaziland and Zimbabwe. A standardized household questionnaire, protocols for sampling and all other aspects of data collection and processing were collaboratively developed by SAMP partners. In addition to queries about migrant destinations, occupations and demographics, questions were asked about remittance behaviour, the methods used for remittance transfer, the role of remittances in the migrant-sending household economy, and the impact of migrant remittances on migrant-sending households.

The Migration and Remittances Survey (or MARS) is national-scale and statistically representative. Households were randomly selected and included in the survey if they answered 'yes' to the question: 'Are there migrants who work outside this country living in this household?' A total of 4,700 households were identified in the regional sample. The Lesotho portion of the sample consisted of 1,023 households. Data was collected on household attributes as well as the characteristics of individual household members, both migrants and non-migrants. Information was gathered on a total of 1,076 migrants of whom 899 were male and 177 were female.

Only migrant-sending households were included in the survey. Migrants 'away' in South Africa (or other countries) were not themselves interviewed. Instead, data on their migration and remittance practices and demographic characteristics was obtained from household members in Lesotho. Furthermore, the households captured in the data set were those reporting members working outside the country, and thus excluded either migrants who were not working or migrants who had not left household members behind in their home countries. The data thus reflects the situation for economic migrants: people who live away from home for reasons related to their employment or occupation.

In order to explore remittance behaviour and its impact in greater depth, individual and focus group case-study research was conducted in Lesotho. All interviews, including those with migrants, were conducted in Lesotho because of the difficulties of identifying a sufficient number of migrants within South Africa and the fact that migrants would be more likely to give honest answers when at home than if they were interviewed in a foreign country where many work illegally. Most migrants come home for the festive season in December, which meant there were no problems in identifying interviewees.

A semi-structured questionnaire was prepared to provide basic data on household demography, income, and remittance information. Respondents were then asked to elaborate on their perceptions of the importance of migration, household decision-making on migration and the impact of migration to South Africa on the household and the community. Five focus groups were conducted (two with migrants, two with remittance receivers and one with remittance-based entrepreneurs). All interviews were conducted in Sesotho and transcribed and translated into English for analysis.

PAST MIGRATIONS

Over the course of the twentieth century, the people of Lesotho became deeply reliant on migration to South Africa.[10] An extensive research literature in the 1970s and 1980s showed that circular migration between Lesotho and South Africa had an impact on all aspects of Basotho economic, social and cultural life: dividing families, weakening domestic social structure and organization, undermining agricultural production and productivity, compromising health, exacerbating rural poverty and intensifying gender inequality.[11] Migration was consistently seen as having a relentlessly negative impact on development, an interpretation of the migration-development relationship that persists to the present. Lesotho was once the "granary" of Southern Africa, the home of a productive agricultural peasantry producing crops for export but was reduced over time to an impoverished labour reserve for South African industry. The central question for these researchers was not "Why are the Basotho still poor?" but rather "How have the Basotho become poor?"[12]

The historical and contemporary dependence of households in Lesotho on migration to South Africa was recently described by Turner as follows:

> For generations, Basotho livelihood aspirations have focused on wage employment. For most of this time, the country's role as a regional labour reserve meant that most of this wage employment was across the border in South Africa. To have at least one wage earner in the family is seen as the foundation of livelihood security, both through current wage income and through future activities. These future activities (notably farming) can be built from the assets that wages may buy, and may continue long after wage earning has ceased. Poverty threatens households that are unable to break into wage employment, or that lose such employment permanently.[13]

The inter-generational character of migration from Lesotho to South Africa was corroborated by the MARS, which found that 76% of Basotho respondents (household heads or their partners) had parents and at least 25% had grandparents who had worked in South Africa. This compared to a regional average of 57% and 23% (Table 1).

Table 1: Migration Experience of Parents and Grandparents		
	Lesotho	Region*
Parent Worked in Another Country (%)		
Yes	76.2	57.1
No	15.7	34.7
Don't Know	8.1	8.2
	100.0	100.0
Grandparent Worked in Another Country (%)		
Yes	24.4	22.6
No	21.1	43.3
Don't Know	54.5	34.2
Total	100.0	100.0
Source: SAMP Household Survey		
* Includes Botswana, Lesotho, Mozambique, Swaziland, Zimbabwe		

During the twentieth century, the major form of legal movement between Lesotho and South Africa was contract migration for work on the South African gold mines. Lesotho (along with Malawi and Mozambique) became a major supply source for the mines.[14] The number of migrants increased over time and reached nearly 130,000 at the peak in 1990 (Table 2). Almost 50% of households in Lesotho had at least one household member working as a migrant on the South African mines in the late 1970s. Migrants signed contracts of up to a year in length and spent a good part of their working lives away from home. Most migrants were young, single men who aimed to return permanently to Lesotho once they had accumulated sufficient stock and savings to marry and establish their own household. Their sons, when old enough, would take their place on the mines.

Mine work is extremely demanding both physically and mentally.[15] Not all men were suited to, or capable of, working underground. Some therefore migrated to South Africa to work in other sectors such as manufacturing and construction. But mining overshadowed all other forms of migrant employment. In 1975, for example, 81% of migrants worked in mining, 7.5% were in manufacturing, 5% in domestic work (mainly women), 3% in construction, 2% in government and 1% in agriculture.[16]

Table 2: Migration of Miners from Lesotho to South Africa, 1920-2005		
Year	Average No. Employed	Actual No. of Recruits (Est.)
1920	10,439	15,000
1925	14,256	20,000
1930	22,306	30,000
1935	34,778	36,000
1940	52,044	55,000
1945	36,414	36,000
1950	34,467	35,000
1955	36,332	38,000
1960	48,842	53,000
1965	54,819	57,000
1970	63,998	70,000
1975	78,114	83,000
1980	96,309	100,000
1985	97,639	100,000
1990	99,707	127,000
1995	87,935	97,000
2000	58,224	64,000
2005	46,069	48,000
Source: TEBA		

During the apartheid era, Basotho miners were not allowed by South African law to stay in the country beyond the length of their contracts and they could not bring their spouses or families with them. At work they lived in regimented single-sex barracks known as compounds or hostels. They sent home a significant proportion of their wages as remittances, but still not enough in the view of the post-colonial Lesotho government. In 1974, the government therefore passed the Lesotho Deferred Pay Act (Act No. 18), which established a compulsory remittance system.[17]

In the stereotypical view, men migrated to work on the South African mines and women were forced to remain behind to tend the fields and raise the family.[18] This was certainly the experience of many women but by no means all. Female migration to South Africa was never as voluminous as male migration, but nor was it entirely absent. From the early twentieth century, female migrants from Lesotho were usually young women or widows escaping poverty at home.[19] The decision to migrate was often taken out of desperation. As Murray observed in 1981: "Despite the degrading conditions, social isolation and risk of arrest … women go because they have no alternative."[20] In South Africa, they were highly marginalized in the labour market and often confined to domestic service or to illegal informal sector activity including brewing and sex work.

The ability of Basotho women (and non-mine male migrants) to seek work in South Africa was curtailed by the South African Aliens Control Act of 1963. Prior to that time, migrants from Lesotho could cross freely and work in South Africa. After 1963, passports, residence and work permits were required. Legal employment in South Africa became very difficult for Basotho women. Only the South African mining companies were exempted from the legislation. The number of female migrants from Lesotho in South Africa fell quickly during the 1960s.

Changing Patterns of Migration Since 1990

Since 1990, there have been major shifts in the nature of migration from Lesotho to South Africa. The most significant changes include:
- Greatly increased cross-border movement between Lesotho and South Africa
- Declining employment opportunities for Basotho men in the South African gold mines
- Increased female migration from Lesotho
- Growing internal female migration of young women within Lesotho
- Increases in skilled migration from Lesotho
- Growth of AIDS-related migration in Lesotho

Increased Cross-Border Movement

The number of people crossing the border legally through the official border posts between Lesotho and South Africa increased dramatically after 1990, rising from 240,000 in 1991 to over 2 million in 2007. Lesotho is easily the most important source of African entrants into South Africa, sending a quarter or more of the total since the early 1990s (Table 3; Figure 1).[21]

Not all of those who cross from Lesotho to South Africa are migrants going to work or to engage in income-generating activity. In the late 1990s, SAMP asked a nationally representative sample of adults in Lesotho the reason for their most recent visit to South Africa. By far the majority (34%) had gone to visit family or friends. Another 19% had gone to shop. Only 17% had gone to work, with another 8% to look for work. Other reasons included medical treatment (6%), trading (3%), tourism (2%), business (2%) and study (1%).[22] In other words, only a quarter of cross-border movements were employment-related.

Table 3: Legal Migration from Lesotho to South Africa, 1991-2009			
Year	Africa	Lesotho	% Lesotho
1991	1,193,743	243,710	20.4
1992	2,327,959	887,811	38.1
1993	2,700,415	1,038,479	38.5
1994	3,125,959	1,184,893	37.9
1995	3,452,164	1,097,351	31.8
1996	3,781,351	1,189,129	31.4
1997	3,665,003	1,190,848	32.5
1998	4,291,547	1,649,511	38.4
1999	4,353,259	1,588,365	36.5
2000	4,298,613	1,559,422	36.3
2001	4,193,732	1,288,160	30.7
2002	4, 513,694	1,162,786	25.8
2003	4,519,616	1,291,242	28.6
2004	4,707,384	1,479,802	31.4
2005	5,446,062	1,668,826	30.6
2006	6,308,636	1,919,889	30.4
2007	6,902,041	2,171,954	31.5
2008	7,395,414	2,165,505	29.3
Source: Statistics South Africa			

Figure 1: Legal Migration from Lesotho to South Africa, 1991-2009

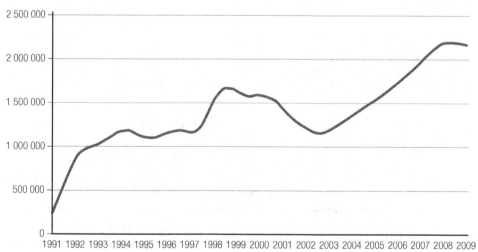

The hyper-mobility of the population of contemporary Lesotho, and the complex connections between internal and international migration, are captured in the following description:

The Basotho are integrated together in a fluid shifting ensemble of people, where members of the same family may have a relative managing sheep and goats in the upper Senqu Valley in Lesotho, while his brother cultivates mountain wheat and keeps a home ready for the herdsman when he comes down for the winter. They have a sister who has married in the lowlands, where she struggles to grow maize on an exhausted piece of eroded land. Her husband is fortunate to work in the South African mines, and comes home monthly. When he was younger he brought cattle back home from the mines, but now as he has grown older he prefers to bring money and household goods. The sheep and goat herder in the mountain has a cousin who teaches school in a peri-urban community near Mafeteng and another cousin who works in a textile factory in Maputsoe. She married a policeman in Bloemfontein, South Africa, and is waiting until he finds a place for both of them so she can move there. A distant uncle in Bloemfontein who took permanent residence in South Africa when he retired from the mines is helping them find a place to live. All of these folk visit each other regularly, so that there is a constant flow from mountain to lowland to town to South African city and back.[23]

DECLINING MINE MIGRATION

During the 1990s, a stagnant gold price led to a major period of declining production, mine closures and retrenchments in South Africa's low-grade gold mines.[24] In 1990, there were around 376,000 migrant miners in the industry. By 2004, there were only 230,000: a total job loss of 140,000. Of those who were left, around 50,000 (about a sixth) were from Lesotho (Table 4). Between 1995 and 2006, the proportion of Basotho miners in the total workforce fell from 30% to 17%.

The impact of retrenchments on so many migration-dependent households in Lesotho was devastating.[25] When 50,000 miners lost their jobs, almost as many households lost their main source of income. The proportion of households in Lesotho with at least one household member working as a migrant on the South African mines declined to only 12% in 2002 from 50% twenty years earlier.[26] Young male school-leavers could no longer rely on migration to the South African gold mines for employment, as they had for decades. Mine employment became an elusive goal for men: "What used to be the absolute economic backbone of Basotho villages and rural economies has been degraded into the privilege of a few."[27]

After 2001, the increase in the gold price halted the dramatic decline of the South African gold industry and employment levels increased once again.[28] However, the number of migrant miners from Lesotho continued to fall (from 58,000 in 2000 to 46,000 in 2006) (Table 4). Under pressure from the South African government to employ more locals, the mining companies met their needs by hiring internal migrants from within South Africa. According to the National Union of Mineworkers, no new workers ('novices') have been recruited from Lesotho since 2002.[29]

Table 4: Mine Jobs in South Africa for Basotho Migrants (Average No. Employed)			
Year	Basotho Workers	Total Workers	% Basotho
1990	99,707	376,473	26.5
1991	93,897	354,649	26.5
1992	93,519	339,485	27.5
1993	89,940	317,456	28.3
1994	89,237	315,264	28.3
1995	87,935	291,902	30.1
1996	81,357	284,050	28.6
1997	76,361	262,748	29.1
1998	60,450	228,071	26.5
1999	52,188	213,832	24.4
2000	58,224	230,687	25.2
2001	49,483	207,547	23.8
2002	54,157	234,991	23.0
2003	54,479	234,027	23.3
2004	48,962	230,771	21.2
2005	46,049	236,459	19.5
2006	46,082	267,894	17.2
Source: TEBA			

The absence of "new blood" is reflected in the age profile of Basotho miners. In 2005, MARS found that less than 3% of miners were under the age of 25 and less than 11% were under 30 (Table 5). Over half of the miners were over the age of 40 and 20% were over the age of 50. Nearly 70% of the miners had over 10 years experience working on the gold mines and around 30% had more than 20 years experience. This represents a major shift from the past: historically, the majority of miners were in their twenties and thirties and expected to retire from this back-breaking work once they were in their forties and their adult sons could take their place.

Table 5: Age of Migrant Miners		
Age Group	No.	%
20-24	26	2.8
25-29	73	7.9
30-34	106	11.5
35-39	187	20.3
40-44	176	19.1
45-49	162	17.6
50-54	116	12.6
55-59	47	5.1
60-64	20	2.3
>65	7	0.8
Total	920	100.0
Source: SAMP Household Survey		

The decline in gold mine employment has had two spin-off impacts on migration from Lesotho: (a) a diversification in patterns of labour migration as new migrants seek out other employment opportunities in post-apartheid South Africa and (b) an increase in female migration to South Africa as female household members replace retrenched males and seek employment opportunities in sectors that prefer female employees (such as domestic service and commercial farming).[30]

FEMINIZATION OF MIGRATION

The growing "feminization" of migration from Lesotho has meant (a) an increase in the absolute number of female migrants; (b) an increase in the proportion of migrants who are female; and (c) a qualitative change in the character of female migration. The reasons why more women are migrating include, first, the collapse of apartheid, which made it easier to migrate and to find work without being constantly harassed and deported. Secondly, as one Focus Group participant noted, remaining in Lesotho makes no economic sense:

> More women are migrating to South Africa because of the difficulties they experience in life and also because the jobs in South Africa offer more money when compared to what we get in Lesotho for the same work we do in South Africa. For domestic work in Lesotho, a woman gets M250 per month whereas in South Africa the minimum they get would be M900.[31]

Once in South Africa, women gravitate to Gauteng because wages there are higher for the same job than they are in nearby Free State towns.[32] The "difficulties" cited as reasons for migration include poverty, hunger, landlessness, unemployment, widowhood or abandonment, supporting AIDS orphans, and no money for school fees, medical treatment or clothing.

Migration within Southern Africa is still male-dominated (Table 6). This is true even in Lesotho, which has seen drastic shrinkage of male migrant labour to the mines. Female migrants from Lesotho make up a higher proportion of the total than in either Swaziland or Mozambique, the two countries with which it can meaningfully be compared.

Table 6: Sex of Migrants		
Country	Male (%)	Female (%)
Lesotho	83.6	16.4
Mozambique	93.6	6.2
Swaziland	92.4	7.6
Zimbabwe	56.4	43.6
Total	84.5	15.5
N	3,972	731
Source: SAMP Household Survey		

Data from several national household surveys between 1990 and 2004, conducted by Sechaba Consultants, provide a general "snapshot" of gender trends at the aggregate level. Table 7 gives the percentage of household members aged 16 and over who were at home, living away from home in Lesotho, and living in South Africa at the time of the particular survey.

Table 7: Geographical Location of Total Adult Population, 1990-2004											
Year	In home community				Elsewhere in Lesotho				Outside Lesotho			
	Subsistence		Other		Working		Other		Mining		Other	
	M %	F %	M %	F %	M %	F %	M %	F %	M %	F %	M %	F %
1990	15	33	17	14	2	1	2	2	11	0	2	1
1993	12	32	20	16	2	2	2	2	9	0	2	2
1999	14	29	23	13	2	2	2	2	4	0	3	2
2004	19	29	17	17	2	3	1	2	3	0	3	3
Source: Sechaba Consultants											

In 2004, compared to the early 1990s, the proportion of adults who were at home increased (from 32% to 36%) while women decreased fractionally (47% to 46%). The proportion who were men involved in subsistence activities at home increased (from 15% to 19%) and those who were women decreased (from 33% to 29%). The proportion of men who were away from home but still in Lesotho declined from 4% to 3% (although the proportion actually working remained virtually steady at 2%). The proportion who were women away from home increased from 4% to 8% (and those working from 2% to 6%). International migration trends show a marked decline in male migration (from 13% to 6% of the population) and increase in female migration (from 1% to 3%). The male decrease is particularly marked in the case of mine migrants (from 11% to 3%). Thus, while male migration flows out of the country are still larger than female, the gap has been closing.

The recent feminization in migration from Lesotho is indicated by the fact that nearly 60% of female migrants have less than five years migratory experience (compared with 29% of men) (Figure 2). Over 80% of women have been migrating for ten years or less. At the other end of the scale, a quarter of male migrants have over 20 years migration experience (compared to only 6.8% of female migrants).

Figure 2: Length of Experience as Migrant Worker (%)

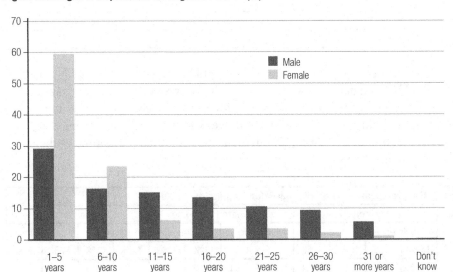

MARS found a much less significant gender difference in the age of migrants (Table 8). The 'middle' age cohort of 25 to 39 contains the most migrants amongst women, while for men it is the older, 40-59 range. The proportion of female migrants falling into the younger 15-24 age bracket is also higher than the equivalent proportion for males. However, the differences are not large. For both men and women, migration now appears to be practised at all stages of the life course, rather than as a temporary measure at a young age, as in the past. The presence of female migrants across the full age range is also consistent with the large numbers of female migrants from Lesotho whose marital status is widowed or separated, and who therefore depend on their own migration for their livelihood.

Table 8: Age of Migrants		
Age Group	Males (%)	Females (%)
15 to 24	5.4	9.7
25 to 39	41.6	41.3
40 to 59	47.3	37.2
60 and over	3.1	4.1
Don't know	2.6	7.7
Total	100	100
N	934	196
Source: SAMP Household Survey		

Gender differences in migration from Lesotho are clearly shaped by household structure and roles. Overall, the household survey showed that male migrants are most likely to be in the 'married' category, while female migrants are for the most part without husbands, either because they have not yet or never married, or because their husbands have left them or died (Table 9). A much higher proportion of female migrants are unmarried compared to their male counterparts: 25% of female migrants compared to just below 10% of male migrants. This suggests that some women, whether by choice or necessity, are selecting migration over marriage as their primary means of economic support, or at least are delaying marriage until later in life. Among male migrants, 84% are married, whereas the equivalent figure for female migrants is only just above a quarter (with 48% once married).

Table 9: Marital Status of Migrants		
Marital Status	Males (%)	Females (%)
Unmarried	9.7	25.0
Married	84.2	26.5
Cohabiting	0.3	0.5
Divorced	0	4.6
Separated	1.7	15.3
Abandoned	0.2	3.6
Widowed	3.9	24.5
Total	100	100
N	934	196
Source: SAMP Household Survey		

Another important finding is the high proportion of female migrants giving their position in the family as 'daughter.' Over 50% of female migrants are younger members of households; either daughters, daughters-in-law or nieces compared to only 22% of male migrants who are sons, sons-in-law or nephews. This confirms the new post-1990 trend, where young women are engaging in economic migration practices once associated mainly with young men.

As significant are the differences between male and female migrants in levels of separation, divorce, abandonment and widowhood. Almost half of the female migrants from Lesotho fall into these categories, compared to only around 6% of the male migrants. This suggests that marital breakdown or loss of a husband act as significant drivers of female migration. Whatever the circumstances leading to the loss of a male partner, these women are often the primary or sole breadwinners for their families in what have become female-headed households. One widow described how her daughter's separation had forced her to migrate:

> My daughter was married, but is now separated. She had to migrate due to problems in her household. Her husband was not prepared to settle the dispute they had. Their children were dying of hunger and she asked me permission to leave. I see her migration as helping me because I no longer have means. She is really helping me. Things were getting tough for me. The going would be very tough without the money. Being that little, I can only use it for a few things.[33]

Her daughter has been working for three years as a domestic worker in South Africa where she earns around R10,000 a year, remitting about R3,000 back to her mother and two children who stay with the mother.

The incidence of female widowhood, divorce and separation in the Lesotho sample was not only higher than for men, but also dramatically higher than the levels reported for female migrants in any of the other countries surveyed. The fact that the unmarried, married, widowed and divorced/separated/abandoned categories each contained roughly equivalent proportions of the total number of female migrants from Lesotho is of fundamental importance in understanding the nature and impact of female migrants' remittances, including who receives their remittances and how those remittances are spent.

The high incidence of widowhood and separation is further reflected in the proportion of women migrants (24%) who are heads of households (Table 10). This reinforces the suggestion that female migration and female household headship are causally linked. The absence of a male household head appears to encourage female migration, whether because of the lack of local livelihood or employment options for women, or due to the absence of patriarchal restriction on women's migration by a male spouse.

Table 10: Relationship of Migrants to Household Head		
Relation	Males (%)	Females (%)
Head	76.5	24.0
Spouse/partner	0.1	18.4
Son/daughter	21.8	45.4
Father/mother	0.0	1.0
Brother/sister	0.5	1.5
Grandchild	0.4	1.5
Grandparent	0.0	0.0
Son/daughter-in-law	0.1	5.1
Nephew/niece	0.0	0.5
Other relative	0.6	2.6
Non-relative	0.0	0.0
Total	100	100
N	934	196
Source: SAMP Household Survey		

In the past, most male migrants were young single men. As many as three-quarters of male migrants are now household heads compared to 25% of female migrants. While the female figure is much lower, it does indicate that a sizable group of women not only have the responsibility of being the head of their own household but must also migrate out of the country to ensure the survival of the household.

Becoming 'South African'

I am a single mother with two sons aged 18 and 7 in Lesotho. Both of my parents are dead and I decided to go to work in South Africa to earn money to feed my sons and to put my children through school. I have been migrating to South Africa for nine years and I spend eleven months away at a time. While I am away my two sons look after themselves. It is not a good thing as my children remain here alone when I am at work and that I don't like at all. I earn R14,000 a year as a domestic and I send my sons around R6,000 a year because I don't pay transport, rent or buy food at work.

The money is still better than it was in the (textile) factories and the working conditions are good. I send the money home through a bank. My older son gets the money from the bank in

Lesotho and the two boys use the money for food, rent, clothing and school fees.

I make a little extra through membership of a stokvel (money company). I contribute R150 a month. The stokvel loans out money to its members and to others. The capital and profits are divided between the members at the end of the year to buy groceries for Christmas holidays.

I have a South African passport so I do not need to return to Lesotho to renew a permit. I am also treated well unlike how they treat other Africans from other countries. I no longer even use my Lesotho passport. I will keep going to South Africa as long as there is work. However, I am also thinking of going to South Africa with my two children. I have more benefits available to me as a South African citizen and it would also be easier for me to have my own house.

EXPANSION OF INTERNAL FEMALE MIGRATION

Female migration to South Africa would be even more voluminous if it was not for the dramatic growth in local employment opportunities in Lesotho's textile industry. The industry started in the late 1980s when Asian (primarily Taiwanese) investors relocated from South Africa to Lesotho to avoid sanctions on South Africa and to access the European market under the Lome Convention.[34] In the 1990s, the industry continued to grow as new overseas markets were developed to take advantage of Lesotho's unmet quotas under the Multifiber Arrangement (MFA) of the General Agreement on Tariffs and Trade. The industry was stimulated after 2000 by Lesotho's privileged status as a duty-free exporter to the US under that country's Africa Growth and Opportunities Act (AGOA).[35] The Act gave Lesotho-based textile producers privileged access to the US garment market. Lesotho could also import fabrics from Asia under AGOA for use in garment manufacture. Between 2000 and 2004, textile exports more than doubled, the number of factories rose to 47 and the workforce to 50,000. Virtually all of the factories were foreign-owned, the majority by Taiwanese investors. Over 90% of exports went to the US.

The phasing out of quotas maintained under the WTO Agreement on Textile and Clothing in January 2005 caused a crisis in the Lesotho industry. Exports fell, factories shut down as their owners (no longer constrained by quota restrictions) relocated to Asia, and thousands of jobs were lost (an estimated 15,000 in 2005-6 alone). The Lesotho

Government responded by granting further concessions to producers and securing "ethical buying" contracts with major US buyers such as The Gap, Walmart and Levi Strauss.[36] By mid-2006, the industry had rebounded with factories re-opening and employment levels once again reaching almost 50,000. The changing fortunes of the industry are evident in production figures for the period 1992 to 2005 (Figure 3).

From the beginning, the textile companies preferred female to male labour.[37] Female workers are considered more "docile" and "nimble" by employers. They are certainly ultra-exploitable.[38] Today, over 90% of Basotho employed in textile factories are young women, most of whom are internal migrants. The numbers have risen even as the number of male mineworkers has fallen, leading some to characterize Basotho female textile workers as the 'new miners' (Figure 4).[39] However, the emerging employment opportunities for young women "have come to a group which is structurally different from that of men, the 'traditional' breadwinners and wage earners."[40]

In many households, young women have displaced young men as the primary wage earners.[41] However, there is a large difference in salary between male miners and female garment workers. In 2002, for example, miners earned an average of M2,900 per month, while garment workers received only M650 per month. The situation was even worse in 2006, when miners were receiving a substantially higher wage of M4,500 a month, while the garment workers' salaries had not changed. The demand for employment in the textile factories far outstrips the supply, providing no incentive to employers to raise wages.[42]

Figure 3: Textile Production in Lesotho

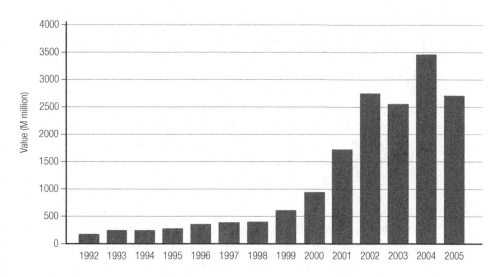

Figure 4: Employment in South African Mines and Lesotho Garment Factories, 1990-2006

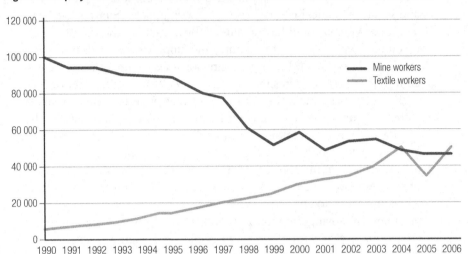

Despite low per capita wages, M225 million was paid to Basotho workers by textile manufacturers in 2002.[43] This doubled to M449 million in 2004.[44] One study claims that "very little is remitted to the family or household."[45] However, a survey of textile workers conducted in 2001 concluded that there is a "significant transfer" of remittances to the poorer areas of Lesotho from which many of the workers come.[46] The average per capita remittance was M139 per month, a total of M50 million per annum. At the time, therefore, these female workers were voluntarily remitting nearly 25% of their earnings to their rural households.

BRAIN DRAIN TO SOUTH AFRICA

After 1990, many skilled Basotho anticipated being able to migrate relatively freely to South Africa for work. This did not happen in the numbers predicted because of South Africa's restrictionist attitude towards all forms of skilled immigration after 1994.[47] Those who did get work permits in South Africa were either exceptionally skilled or had relatives through whom they obtained identity documents (ID's) and residence permits. They were also able to take advantage of the deracialization of the South African workforce and affirmative action programmes: "They have been helped by the fact that Sesotho is an official language of South Africa and many Basotho have been eligible for South African citizenship but it means that Lesotho has often lost many of her most skilled citizens."[48] In the MARS study, around 10% of migrants from Lesotho were found to be working in skilled occupations in South Africa (Table 11). With the exception of supervisory and skilled manual work (primarily mine jobs), the proportion of female migrants in every category (including office work, teaching and health work) was higher than that of male migrants.

Table 11: Skilled Migrant Occupations in South Africa			
	Males %	Females %	Total %
Managerial office worker	0.1	0.5	0.2
Office worker	0.2	0.5	0.3
Supervisor	0.1	0.0	0.1
Skilled manual worker	7.4	4.6	6.2
Professional worker	2.8	4.6	2.9
Teacher	0.1	0.5	0.1
Health worker	0.0	1.5	0.3
Total	10.7	12.5	10.1
Source: SAMP Household Survey			

South Africa's 2002 Immigration Act has made it easier for skilled migrants to work in South Africa and the numbers of skilled Basotho working in South Africa has risen accordingly. This brain drain to South Africa is very likely to accelerate in the future.[49] A SAMP survey of final year students in Lesotho's technical colleges and the National University of Lesotho showed that interest in leaving Lesotho, either temporarily or permanently, is very high.[50] Nearly a third of the students (31%) believed they would end up working in South Africa. Other destinations mentioned included Botswana (25%), the United Kingdom (10%), Europe (9%) and the USA (7%).

HIV/AIDS AND MIGRATION

There is a significant body of research in Southern Africa that identifies population mobility as one of the major reasons for the rapid transmission of the disease throughout the region.[51] Certainly, its spread in Lesotho in the 1990s cannot be explained without taking account of the extraordinary mobility of the population.[52] The spread of HIV and AIDS has not simply been fuelled by migration. Migration, by its very nature, facilitates high-risk behaviour and makes migrants more vulnerable to HIV infection.

The first identified case of HIV infection in Lesotho was in 1986. Initially, growth in HIV prevalence was slow, only reaching 0.04% in 1990. For the next eight years, the rise was rapid, climbing from an estimated 1.0% in 1991 to 30.5% in 1998 and to 37% in 2008. Data from antenatal clinics show a rise in prevalence amongst pregnant women in the country's main city, Maseru, from 5.5% in 1991 to 42.2% in 2000.[53] The Lesotho Behavioural Surveillance Survey (2002) conducted interviews with miners, taxi-drivers and assistants, soldiers, low-income migrant women (working in Lesotho, mainly in the textile industry) and female sex workers.[54] Despite widespread knowledge of the causes and prognosis for those with HIV and AIDS, rates of non-regular and multi-partner sex were high amongst all groups, not just sex workers.[55] Condom use was low and sporadic amongst all of these groups of internal and international migrants. A study of the environs of ten border posts between South Africa and Lesotho identified them as sites of "profound risk" where commercial sex is widely available.[56] As the study concludes: "There is exceptional HIV vulnerability at each of the sites investigated, a sociocultural context of casual and commercial sex exacerbated by profound mobility (of) truckers, bus and taxi drivers, traders, soldiers, migrant labourers and transient workers."[57]

On the mines, a culture of macho male sexuality and the availability of commercial sex (often with female migrant sex workers) led to the rapid diffusion of HIV amongst the mine workforce in the 1990s.[58] The introduction of HIV to Lesotho is widely attributed to returning migrant miners infected with the virus while at work: migrant labour to the mines "readily transplants HIV risk from the mining camps to rural Lesotho."[59] Migration, which separates and divides couples for extended periods of time, and accompanying poverty, play a complex but significant role in the sexual behaviour and preferences of migrants and their partners while apart.[60] The death of either partner has profound consequences, as one Focus Group participant observed:

> Let us look at it this way. Some men do not come home
> when they are in South Africa. We may not know the rea-
> sons but many die there and their spouses are forced to go
> and look for jobs in South Africa. While many women go
> to South Africa because of problems in their households the
> risk is, when they fail to get those jobs, they get into sexual
> relations with many men from the mines. They switch into
> prostitution and what then happens is that they contract
> HIV/AIDS. They would be looking for let us say R20 from
> each man and in this way, each woman would be looking
> for five or more men to get R100. The intention is to send
> money back home to the children and leaving something for
> herself to eat. The result of all this is the man dies and she is
> also going to die.[61]

The 2004 Lesotho Demographic and Health Survey tested blood samples from throughout the country and found: (a) prevalence rates were higher for all ages for women than men (b) the peak age range for infection was 30-34 for men and 35-39 for women; (c) after age 40 rates decline with age.[62] Although urban prevalence is higher than rural for both men and women, rural prevalence is still significant (33% versus 24% for women, 22% versus 18.5% for men) (Figure 5, Table 12).

Figure 5: HIV Prevalence Amongst Women at Antenatal Clinics (%)

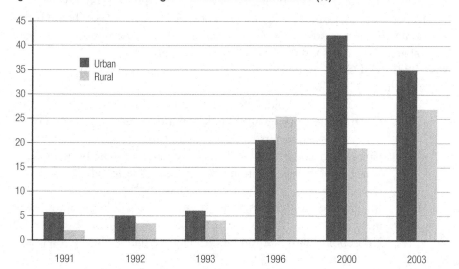

Table 12: National HIV/AIDS Prevalence by Gender, Age and Spatial Distribution			
Age	Women	Men	Total
15-19	7.9	2.3	5.3
20-24	24.2	12.2	19.5
25-29	39.8	23.9	33.3
30-34	39.3	41.1	40.0
35-39	43.3	39.1	41.8
40-44	29.1	33.9	30.6
45-49	16.8	26.2	20.0
Urban	33.0	22.0	29.1
Rural	24.3	18.5	21.9
Lowlands	28.0	20.4	24.9
Foothills	24.2	16.9	21.2
Mountains	23.3	17.6	21.0
Source: Government of Lesotho			

HIV/AIDS is also generating new forms of migration. There is evidence that once migrants become too sick to work, they return home permanently.[63] The loss of income for the family is often devastating when a migrant becomes too sick to earn and remit. The impact is exacerbated by the fact that the burden and cost of care is also borne by the family. The other form of migration on the increase is children's migration as orphans are sent to live with extended family members in different parts of the country or in South Africa.[64] The HIV/AIDS epidemic has left many farmers unable to do the hard physical labour required to work the land and many migrants without the physical energy or resources to continue to migrate for work. As Turner notes: "There is no doubt that the pandemic will exacerbate poverty as the nation's aggregate capacity to farm is reduced by sickness and death."[65]

HIV/AIDS has a number of implications for households in Lesotho including:

- Increased household dependency ratios. Chronic illness and death in the working age population are increasing the ratio of dependent consumers to producers in the household;
- Changes in household headship. The death of male household heads is increasing the number of widows and female-headed households;
- Incomplete Households. One parent or one whole generation is missing;
- Households with Additional Orphans. Orphans are the responsibility of the next of kin;
- Orphan-Headed Households. These are apparently not as common in Lesotho as elsewhere but are likely to increase in number;
- Defunct Households. When both parents die, there are no resident adults and the children are dispersed to live with relatives.[66]

All of these changes in household structure, division of labour and livelihood strategies are increasing the economic vulnerability of households. Households that experience the death of a migrant from HIV and AIDS generally experience increased poverty.

MIGRANT DESTINATIONS

PURPOSE OF JOURNEY

Migrants from Lesotho go almost entirely to South Africa. MARS found that 99.8% of Basotho migrants work in South Africa and the remainder are in Botswana. South Africa not only has the strongest and most diverse economy in the region, providing a variety of employment and livelihood opportunities, it is also by far the largest and most affluent market for migrants with commodities to sell. In addition, it has the greatest variety of goods for purchase, consumption or trade. The long tradition of labour migration, together with linguistic and cultural traits shared with the South

African population, makes it an accessible and familiar destination.

Why people go to South Africa from Lesotho has a very clear influence on where they go. For example, the majority of people going to purchase goods for their own consumption or trade go to the South African border towns of Ladybrand, Ficksburg and Thaba Nchu/Botsabelo (Table 13). Bloemfontein, the nearest large South African city, is also a popular destination. The primary destinations for those going to work are the mining towns of Welkom and Virginia (24% of all Basotho going to these towns go there to work), Johannesburg (16%) and Bethlehem (14%). Other smaller towns scattered around the Free State and Gauteng Provinces also attract migrants going to work. Those running their own business (mainly informal sector traders) make up 40% of Basotho visitors to Cape Town and 21% of visitors to Johannesburg.

Table 13: South African Destinations by Purpose of Journey

	Shopping	Own business	Leisure	Employer's business	Education	Work	Medical Services	Other	Total
Bethelehem	21.4	35.7	-	14.3	7.1	14.3	-	7.2	100
Bloemfontein	25.4	20.9	17.9	9.0	17.9		6.0	2.9	100
Cape Town	40.0	-	-	20.0	40.0	-	-	-	100
Durban	-	50.0	-	50.0	-	-	-	-	100
Ficksburg	48.5	22.4	6.0	2.4	0.2	5.2	3.7	11.6	100
Johannesburg	2.3	20.9	41.9	7.0	2.3	16.3	-	9.3	100
Ladybrand	60.6	18.9	8.7	6.3	0.8	-	3.9	0.8	100
Pietermaritzburg	-	-	100	-	-	-	-	-	100
Pretoria	-	10.0	10.0	30.0	50.0	-	-	-	100
Harrismith		14.3	28.6	14.3	14.3		14.3	14.4	100
Thaba Nchu	31.6	5.3	26.3	10.5	5.3	5.3		15.7	100
Welkom	1.4	16.9	25.4	15.5	4.2	23.9	4.2	8.5	100
Wepener	-	-	100	-	-	-	-		100
Other FS	6.5	35.5	12.9	9.7	6.5	19.4		9.7	100
Other Gauteng	1.1	19.5	27.6	4.6	3.4	20.7	9.2	13.8	100
Other RSA	3.1	18.8	37.5	21.9	6.3	12.5	-	-	100
Outside RSA	33.3	-	33.3	-	33.4	-	-	-	100

Source: SAMP Household Survey

Overall, minework is still the profession of the majority of male Basotho migrants. The dominant employment sector for female migrants is domestic service (with 50% of female migrants). Overall, women are employed in a wider variety of jobs and sectors than men although no other sector employs more than 10% of female migrants. Another significant difference between male and female migrants lies in self-employment. Only 3% of male migrants but 16% of female migrants are informal sector producers or traders and hawkers. A greater proportion of women migrants also described themselves as self-employed business persons. Finally, while there are proportionally more skilled manual workers who are male, women have a stronger presence than men in most skilled categories including office work, professional work, teaching and the health sector.

SOUTH AFRICAN GOLD MINES

Migrant miners still make up 80% of male migrants to South Africa (Table 14). Mineworkers are recruited (rehired) annually in Lesotho on contract by the mine labour agency TEBA. Before 2002, they were employed under a bilateral agreement between the two governments that dated back to the 1970s. Since the 2002 South Africa Immigration Act came into force, mining companies apply for corporate permits that allow them to employ a certain number of migrants from Lesotho.

Table 14: Migrant Occupations in South Africa			
Main occupation	Males %	Females %	Total %
Farmer	0.1	1.0	0.3
Agricultural worker	1.4	4.6	2.0
Service worker	0.7	3.1	1.1
Domestic worker	0.4	50.0	9.0
Managerial office worker	0.1	0.5	0.2
Office worker	0.2	0.5	0.3
Supervisor	0.1	0.0	0.1
Mine worker	79.8	0.2	68.4
Skilled manual worker	7.4	4.6	6.2
Unskilled manual worker	1.6	2.0	1.5
Informal sector producer	2.1	8.7	2.8
Trader/ hawker/ vendor	1.0	7.1	2.0
Security personnel	0.2	0.0	0.2
Business (self-employed)	0.4	5.6	1.2
Professional worker	2.8	4.6	2.9
Teacher	0.1	0.5	0.1
Health worker	0.0	1.5	0.3
Pensioner	0.1	0.0	0.1
Shepherd	0.6	0.0	0.5
Don't know	0.7	3.1	1.0
Total	100.0	100.0	100.0
Source: SAMP Household Survey			

The majority of today's migrant miners have many years of experience working on the mines. The survey showed that 90% are married and 85% are household heads. The remainder are sons of the household (some married, some unmarried).

Working conditions in the South African mining industry have been examined in depth in a number of studies.[67] Pay is low although the average wage increased from R12,000 per annum in 1992 to R53,000 in 2007. Two thirds of miners spend 11 months of the year away from Lesotho. Working conditions remain extremely dangerous and death and disability are a constant threat. Extensive sub-contracting has led to a deterioration in the working conditions and standards at many mines.[68] Migrants are still compelled to defer up to a third of their wages to Lesotho. Illegal gold mining in disused mines has increased although the working conditions are completely deplorable.[69]

The Rural Aristocracy?

I am 32 years old. I have been working on the South African mines since I was 23. I would never settle in South Africa. I am just there to earn a livelihood for my family. I was unable to find work in Lesotho so my father, who is now deceased, took me to South Africa and managed to find me a mine job. He had been a mineworker when younger and he still had contacts on the mines. I am away in South Africa for 11 months each year and I spend one month back in Lesotho in December and January. I try to return home for a weekend visit at the end of every month but transport to my home is difficult once I arrive in Lesotho.

I am separated from my wife so my mother, who is sick, looks after the family. She makes most of the decisions about how my money (remittances) will be spent. I have two younger sisters. One works in a shop in South Africa but does not send anything. The other looks after the four children. I have two young sons (aged 2 and 4) and also have two nieces. One is the orphaned child of my other sister and one is a child that my late father adopted. There are also two unrelated young men in the household, both of whom are unemployed.

I earn R48,000 a year. R18,000 is sent by Teba (compulsory deferred pay) and I send a further R6,000 which I usually bring myself. I also buy goods in South Africa for the household, especially clothing for the children, and bring them home with me. Last year most of the money I sent was spent on food, clothing, transport, building a house and special events. The rest was spent on medical expenses, fuel, alcohol and tobacco. Since my mother got sick, I also pay someone to hoe her field. I paid for the funeral of a cousin and provided food for an uncle. He has no other source of income. Once all of the household expenses are covered, there is very little.

COMMERCIAL FARMS

The commercial farms of the neighbouring Free State province of South Africa are another important destination for migrants seeking work.[70] MARS found that 5% of female migrants and 1.4% of male migrants are farm workers (Table 14). Most of the migrants are hired on contract in Lesotho, although some come across the border and seek work on their own. A SAMP study of migration to the farms found that:

- The migrants had worked on Free State farms for 1 to 24 seasons, with the majority being recent employees. Males were more recent additions to the farm workforce, averaging 2.4 seasons as opposed to 3.7 for women. Eighty-five percent of males had worked for 3 or less years compared with 66% of females;
- Female migrant workers are significantly older than the men. In the main, female farm workers are older women (often widowed or divorced). Young men with no mine experience seem to be more inclined to take farm work than their mine-experienced, older counterparts;
- About half of all farm workers are married. However, many more men are single (31% compared to 7% of women), while many more women are widowed (26% compared to 3% of men). About 40% are heads of household: 53% of male respondents and 28% of female respondents;
- Both male and female farm workers have limited formal education and few alternative employment opportunities. Roughly 11% have no formal schooling.[71]

Farm workers are drawn from the most marginalized segments of Basotho society. The majority (around 60%) are the only wage earners in their households, despite this income being low-wage and primarily seasonal. When not working as seasonal farm labourers, 31% are unemployed and engage in no income generating activity. Some women undertake supplementary informal sector activity such as selling vegetables (12.5%), beer brewing (5.3%), piece work (4.6%), herding (3.3%), carrying parcels (2.7%) and sewing (2%). Only 24% of respondents reported having a regular (as opposed to seasonal) wage earner in their household.

The majority of Lesotho migrants on Free State farms are hired as seasonal workers (some 83% work for 4 months or less at a time). The rest work between 5 and 12 months per year but are not necessarily employed by only one farmer since they seek work on other farms once their initial contracts expire. Working conditions on the farms are highly onerous and poorly rewarded. Migrants work for an average of 10 hours per day, 6.5 days per week during the season. Many work split shifts or until everything in the fields or factory is harvested or packaged. This means an inconsistent and unpredictable workday – perhaps 5 hours one day and 13 the next.

The general pattern for those harvesting is to begin at about 5 a.m., break for brunch mid-morning and work an afternoon shift until all the produce is harvested. In peak season this pattern is extended and work sometimes continues until midnight. In the processing factories, workers tend to work two 5-hour shifts with 5 hours in between. The working day begins at 5 or 6 a.m. and only ends at 8 or 9 p.m. The average monthly income for farmworkers in 2000 was R225.29 with the highest paid earning R600 per month. Others were earning as little as R60 per month.

Factory to Farm

I am 32 years old. I work on asparagus farms in the eastern Free State. At first I worked in the factories in Lesotho but it was unbearable. The man in charge of the recruitment would gather stones and throw them at us and those who caught the stones were the ones who were employed and the rest would go back home.

I work on the farms because there are no jobs in Lesotho and with the little that I get, I am able to attend to almost all the basic needs of my family, my husband and one child. I work for 8 hours a day, seven days a week. I earn R20 a week and I am paid every Monday. My wages are calculated on an hourly basis. The South Africans and Basotho earn the same wages so there is no conflict between us.

When I am looking for farm work, I go straight to the farms I have worked on before and do not wait to be recruited in Lesotho although it is illegal to enter into South Africa with a purpose of working without a contract. The passports of all the farm workers are kept by our supervisors so that we will not leave the farm. Our movement is restricted for security purposes.

I would want to work in Lesotho. The Government of Lesotho must create jobs for me and my fellow migrants who are forced to go to South Africa to work.

DOMESTIC WORK

The most important occupation for female migrants is the South African domestic service sector. Fifty percent of the migrants are domestic workers (Table 14). The majority are relatively new entrants to the labour market, especially when compared to migrant miners (Figure 6). Only 23% of miners have five or less years of migratory experience, compared to 54% of domestic workers. Eighty one percent of domestic workers have 10 or less years of experience compared to only 39% of miners.

Figure 6: Length of Migration Experience by Occupation

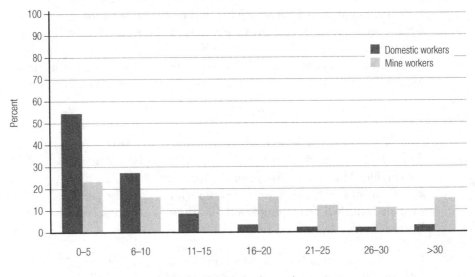

Domestic workers in South Africa are amongst the most poorly paid employees in the country: with 96% earning less than R1,000 per month in 2004 (Table 15). In contrast, 90% of mineworkers earn more than R1,000 a month (and 57% earn more than R2,500 a month). This means that the earning power of most female migrants from Lesotho is much lower than that of their male counterparts.

The South African government recognizes that the working conditions and incomes of domestic workers are poor and has taken steps to improve and regulate their employment standards. In 2006, the official minimum wage for domestic workers employed in urban areas and working more than 27 hours per week was set at R861.90 per month. Maximum working hours were set at 45 hours per week plus ten hours of overtime (nine hours per day for those working 1-5 days per week and eight hours a day for those working 6-7 days per week). Employers of domestic workers also have to make contributions to the Unemployment

Insurance Fund. All of these regulations can easily be avoided by employers if they employ irregular migrants from Lesotho.

Table 15: Monthly Earnings by Sector, South Africa, 2004			
Sector	R1-1000 (%)	R1000-2500 (%)	>R2500 (%)
Agriculture, hunting, forestry and fishing	85.2	4.7	10.1
Community, social and personal services	20.4	10.7	68.9
Construction	58.0	22.2	19.8
Financial intermediation, insurance, real estate and business	30.0	15.5	54.5
Manufacturing	38.0	23.6	38.3
Mining and quarrying	10.1	32.6	57.4
Private households	95.7	3.4	0.9
Transport, storage and communication	28.3	16.7	55.1
Wholesale and retail trade	56.0	17.3	26.7
Source: Labour Force Survey, Sept 2004			

The age and marital profile of migrant domestic workers is very different from that of migrant miners (Table 16). The age spread of migrant domestic workers tends to be broader than that of miners, with a greater proportion of younger migrants. Nearly 22% of domestic workers are under the age of 30 (compared to only 11% of miners). Two-thirds are under the age of 40 (compared to 42% of miners). Again, in contrast to migrant miners, more domestic workers are members of households rather than household heads. The survey found that only 26% of domestic workers are married (compared to 90% of miners) and 24% are household heads (compared to 85% of miners). Exactly the same proportion of domestic workers are unmarried (26.5%) while 43% are daughters of the household and 22% are spouses of household heads. Most striking is that 47% of the domestic workers are widows, separated, divorced or abandoned. In other words, almost half of the migrants are women largely fending for themselves and their dependents. Like migrant miners, the domestic workers also spend the greater part of the year away from Lesotho (87% are away for 11 months at a time). Only 21% get home once a month, 36% only once every six months and 20% once a year.

A SAMP study of the domestic service sector in Johannesburg provides insights into the kinds of conditions experienced by migrants.[72] The working week and day of domestic workers tend to be very long. Over 20% worked a six-day week, and another 20% worked seven days per week. Some 46% worked nine hours or more per day and 31% worked 10 hours or more per day. Some never went off duty. Only 5% of the women had another source of income, which on average brought them in R240 per month.

Table 16: Age of Migrant Domestic Workers	
Age Group	%
15-19	1.5
20-24	6.7
25-29	13.3
30-34	15.6
35-39	20.3
40-44	11.1
45-49	13.3
50-54	12.6
55-59	10.4
>60	8.1
Total	100.0
Source: SAMP Household Survey	

IRREGULAR MIGRATION

Although migrants from Lesotho would prefer to migrate and work legally in South Africa, there are considerable barriers to doing so. Overseas visitors to South Africa are automatically given 90-day temporary residence permits, while legal entrants from Lesotho are only given 30 days, an attempt to discourage people from taking employment when in the country. Only migrant miners, who are issued with one-year residence and work permits, are assured of their legal status. However, if they lose their job they are expected to return immediately to Lesotho.

Most semi-skilled and unskilled migrants from Lesotho are in an irregular work situation because it is impossible to get work permits from the South African authorities. This is particularly true for migrant women in the domestic service sector. Male migrants working in industries such as construction also generally work irregularly. Irregularity exposes migrants to exploitation and abuse and gives them little recourse to the police or justice system. As the Director of Immigration in Lesotho observed about migrant construction workers:

> They get employed as casual labourers. Because of 2010 (Soccer World Cup), there are a number of constructions going on. In the case of casual undocumented labourers, they are underpaid, work long hours for less pay and at times their employers inform the police about them when it is time to pay them and they have to run away leaving their wages behind.[73]

The Director of Consular Affairs in the Department of Foreign Affairs claimed that this was a deliberate strategy by employers to avoid having to pay for work performed:

> There are a few types of these informal job opportunities, namely domestic service and construction. Those who are not lucky face challenges such as not being paid. Most of the construction company owners are involved in many businesses, and to boost those that are lagging behind, they use the resources from those that are vibrant. These people are mostly respected in the townships (by black South Africans) and they use that influence to chase away the Basotho employees at the end of the month when they are supposed to be paid. They call locals to come and chase away Basotho or call the police to inform them that there are illegal immigrants in the area. Basotho are usually forced to leave without being paid.[74]

The Director of Immigration confirmed that female domestic workers face similar treatment:

> We are aware of the agencies such as Household Helpers that hire domestic servants to go and work in South Africa without following proper (legal) channels. This exposes Basotho nationals to exploitation such as the employer keeping their passport to prevent them from going home as they would like to, being underpaid and not enjoying similar benefits as South Africans doing the same jobs.

Irregular employment depresses the wages paid to Basotho migrants, leaving them with less to remit. The apparently widespread practice of "chasing" or "squealing" on casual employees to avoid paying them at month end is a violation of fundamental labour rights but leaves the migrant with nothing to remit at all.

A South African ID makes a great difference to employment prospects, as a female migrant from one Focus Group pointed out:

> Getting to South Africa and staying and working there is not a problem. But it is not easy to access good work in South Africa as almost all migrants don't have South African IDs (Identity Documents). When you have a South African ID, you are able to get better work than people who hold only Lesotho passports. If you are offered a good job, you fail to secure it because you only have a Lesotho passport and end up having to do low-paying jobs such as domestic or shop work. This goes even for those people with high school education.[75]

The value of South African documentation is clearly recognized by migrants. Although fraudulent South African identity and citizenship documentation is always available at a price, some Basotho are able to acquire them through formal application. Basotho in South Africa and Lesotho are ethnically and linguistically homogenous (there are actually more Sesotho-speakers in South Africa than in Lesotho). It is therefore relatively easy to get a direct or distant relative to vouchsafe for the migrant's South African 'roots.'

Does this mean that the "enclave will empty" or that transnational forms of migration will continue or even become more extensive? The evidence suggests that the probability of migrants maintaining strong ties with Lesotho is very high. Nearly two-thirds of the migrants (61%) identified in the household survey return to Lesotho from South Africa at least once a month (compared with a regional average of only 36.3%) (Table 17). A total of 85% return home at least once every three months and 93% at least once every six months. Again, the frequency of personal home visits is much higher than the regional average of 45% every three months and 54% every six months.

Table 17: Frequency of Home Visits		
How often does the migrant come home?	Lesotho (%)	Region (%)
Twice or more per month	1.5	6.2
Once a month	55.6	30.1
More than once in 3 months	9.2	9.0
Once every 3 months	15.2	12.5
Once every 6 months	8.1	9.7
Once a year	8.2	18.5
At end of the contract	0.2	2.6
Other	2.2	11.4
Total	100.0	100.0
Source: SAMP Household Survey		

The Trials of Irregular Migration

I am 23 years old and live in Lesotho with my 71-year-old grandmother who is a widow, and my 37-year-old aunt. She was abandoned by her husband. Also there is my 18-year-old brother and 10-year-old sister. Both of my parents are now dead. I first went to South Africa because my mother and her children were starving. I only have primary education.

I have been away from home for a year. When I left for South

Africa, I got a job with a construction firm. I actually left home not knowing where I would go. All I had decided was to reach any destination where the money I had would allow. I knew that a person never gets lost and indeed I met somebody who I talked to. This person was there for the same reason. I stayed with him. He is also from Lesotho. Ever since I migrated to South Africa, the money I've been earning can only support one person or two at the most. Sometimes there is nothing. It is good that I migrated because there are no jobs in Lesotho and it does not look as if there will be any. Life is still tough.

I earned only R4,800 in my first year as a casual labourer. I sent home R800 which was spent on food, clothing, transport and fuel. The household regularly goes without food. I have recently been joined in South Africa by my brother who is still unemployed. When I crossed the border to South Africa, I was given a 30-day permit. I have to return to the border once a month to renew it. Some people overstay and then they have to pay a bribe to border officials when they eventually return. Others send their passports to the borders with taxi-drivers who get them stamped for a fee and a bribe to the official.

I have money problems especially because employers differ. Sometimes the bosses are reliable, sometimes not. I have worked for many employers who have not paid me yet. Towards the end of the year I took the tools to my boss because he had failed to pay me for some months. I wanted to go home but I had no money. I told my boss that I would take his tools to the office and there he would have to pay me in order to get them. Instead of doing what I asked him to do, he organized some guys to kill me. They beat me very badly, and they would have succeeded had the police not arrived on the scene. My boss told the police that I was a thief, and that he did not know me at all. He participated in the beating. The police wanted to take me away but, battered as I was, I refused to go because I needed my side of the story to be known. I agreed to be taken to my employer (the contractor) but he ultimately ran away. The guys who beat me up again raided my place where I stay. They took my belongings. Another day I was going to the office when I saw them. I was told they had guns. I ran away. Some (South Africans) treat us well and relations are good but some show much hatred to foreigners.

VOLUME AND TYPE OF REMITTANCES

Global remittances have grown to the point where they exceed Official Development Assistance (ODA) and are approaching the level of Foreign Direct Investment (FDI). In Africa as a whole, the picture is rather different with ODA now exceeding FDI. Remittance flows are significantly lower (although data deficiencies are such that the actual flows may be much higher). Lesotho presents a different scenario with remittances being most important, followed by Customs Union Revenue, ODA and finally FDI (Figure 7). Lesotho's major external sources of revenue include:

(a) Southern African Customs Union (SACU) Revenue: SACU governs trade for the member countries of Botswana, Lesotho, Swaziland, Namibia and South Africa. The Union has a common external tariff and guarantees free movement of goods amongst member countries. SACU's revenue-sharing formula has generated a growing proportion of public revenue in Lesotho, rising to M1,107 million in 2003.

(b) Official Development Assistance: Lesotho's ODA inflows fell dramatically after the end of apartheid. After 1999, however, ODA to Lesotho picked up again primarily because of international attention on the impact of the HIV and AIDS epidemic.

(c) Foreign Direct Investment: FDI increased throughout the 1990s with the growth of the textile industry (peaking in 1998) but has fallen by 50% since.

(d) Migrant Remittances: migrant remittances have remained the major revenue source for Lesotho, rising to an estimated M1,939 million in 2004.

Figure 7: Flows of FDI, ODA, Remittances and SACU Revenue to Lesotho

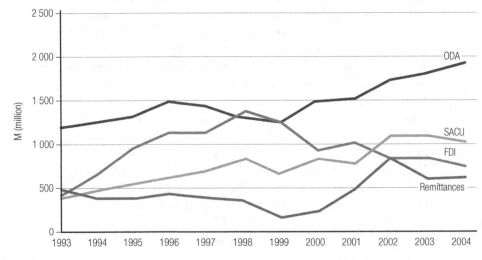

The only completely accurate and reliable data on remittance flows is for compulsory deferred pay (CPD) from the South African mining industry to Lesotho. These remittances are "formal" in that they are channeled through the formal banking system and are captured in official statistics. In 1974, the government passed the Lesotho Deferred Pay Act (Act No. 18 of 1974) which established the legal terms and conditions of a compulsory remittance system for mineworkers.[76] A portion of the miner's wage (initially between 60-90%) was compulsorily deferred and paid into a special account in the Lesotho National Development Bank. Miners received some interest on their deposits, the balance accruing to the government. The funds could only be drawn in Lesotho by the miner himself at the end of a contract. The CDP system ensured that the greater part of a migrant's earnings returned as remittances to Lesotho.

The Deferred Pay Act has been amended several times. A 1979 revision stipulated that 60% of the basic wage would be deposited in Lesotho with the exception of earnings during the first 30 days of employment on a contract. In 1990, the percentage of compulsorily deferred pay was reduced to 30% (excluding the first and last month of the contract). Currently, miners are forced to defer 30% of their gross earnings for 10 months of every 12-month contract. Deferred wages can be accessed by the miner or their bona fide spouse. The recent failure of the Lesotho National Development Bank and widespread dissatisfaction amongst miners with the way the system operated prompted TEBA Bank to reach an agreement with government about taking over the system. TEBA Bank now operates an automated deferred pay system although there is still dissatisfaction amongst miners and their spouses about the way the system runs.

There is a misleading assumption that the decline in employment on the South African mines for Basotho migrants led to a serious decline in remittance flows to Lesotho.[77] In fact, remittances increased over the time period as the total wages paid out to Basotho miners grew from M1,473 million in 1992 to M2,442 million in 2004. The main reason is that the average mine wage increased from M12,000 in 1992 to M53,000 in 2007 (Table 18). The CDP system ensured that Lesotho received a portion of this increase (from M276 million in 1992 to M610 million in 2004). However, the Central Bank of Lesotho estimates that voluntary remittances have also grown (from M1,103 million in 1992 to M1,795 million in 2004). In other words, the Lesotho economy as a whole has not suffered from retrenchments and nor have those households with members still working on the mines. Retrenchments have meant that growing remittance flows are shared by a shrinking number of households. Households who still have a mine worker migrant are clearly better off than those who do not, and constitute something of a "rural aristocracy."

Remittance flows to Lesotho can be classified according to whether they are: (a) compulsory or voluntary; (b) formal or informal (in terms of channels used); and (c) cash or in-kind. Remittances in cash and kind are the main source of income for the vast majority of migrant-sending households in Lesotho. MARS showed that 95% receive regular cash remittances and 20% receive remittances-in-kind (Table 19). Only 9% of the households receive income from regular wage work and 6% from casual work in Lesotho. Additionally, only 9% receive income from a formal or informal business and just 3% from the sale of farm products.

Table 18: Mine Remittances to Lesotho from South Africa				
Year	Total Wages (M million)	Average Annual Wage (M)	Remittances (M million)	CDP (M million)
1992	1473.5	12,321	1103.8	275.9
1993	1551.4	13,359	1104.5	334.4
1994	1641.5	14,562	1170.5	320.0
1995	1743.0	16,801	1242.8	410.6
1996	1951.9	19,186	1391.7	488.0
1997	2032.7	21,193	1321.2	508.2
1998	1996.2	24,678	1217.7	499.1
1999	1897.4	27,657	1157.4	474.4
2000	1955.5	30,131	1394.3	488.9
2001	1966.6	32,030	1402.2	491.7
2002	2196.5	35,236	1594.8	549.1
2003	2364.8	38,513	1686.1	591.2
2004	2442.1	42,116	1795.0	610.5
Source: GOL				

Annualised average household income for migrant-sending households from all sources was M11,475. Mean household income from remittances was M8,400 for cash and M2,488 for goods. Income from other sources was relatively significant for the small number of households that had more diversified income. For example, the 2% of households with a formal business made an average of M6,708 from their business. Or again, the 3% of households selling farm produce made an average of M1,525 from those sales. The 7% of households participating in the informal sector made an average of M3,066 from those operations. In many cases, remittances are not a supplementary form of household income, they are virtually the only form of income.

Figure 8: Mineworker Remittances to Lesotho, 1992-2004

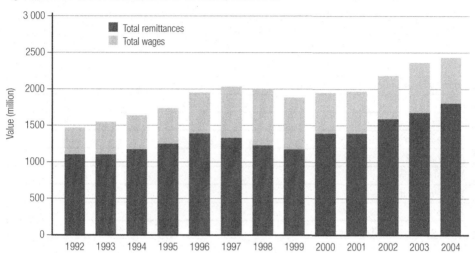

Table 19: Sources of Income of Migrant-Sending Households		
	%	Mean Annual Income (M)
Wage work	9.5	7,420.83
Casual work	6.3	2,618.28
Remittances – money	95.3	10,186.44
Remittances – value of goods	20.0	2,487.70
Income from farm products	2.7	1,525.93
Income from formal business	2.0	6,708.00
Income from informal business	6.8	3,066.41
Pension/disability	0.6	1,025.00
Gifts	2.2	1,178.86
Source: SAMP Household Survey		

There are distinctive differences in remitting patterns by occupation and skill level. Miners remit an average of M10,677 per annum which is more than skilled workers and professionals (M6,260) who, in turn, remit more than other migrants (mainly unskilled women) who remit an average of M3,939 per annum. Female migrant domestic workers in South Africa remit much less than male miners, which is not surprising given the wage differentials between the two sectors. Female domestic workers remit an average of M3,632 per annum (one third the amount of miners). Their remittances are also less frequent than those of miners, most of whom remit once a month or more. Only 42% of domestic workers are able to remit that frequently. Another 20% remit once every 2-3 months and the rest even less often.

In general, households in Lesotho receive remittances frequently and regularly: 78% of households receive cash remittances at least once a month (Table 20). The average annual cash remittance receipt reported by households was M7,800.

Table 20: Frequency of Cash Remittances to Lesotho		
	N	% of HH
Twice or more per month	12	1.2
Once a month	787	76.6
More than twice in 3 months	91	8.9
Once in three months	66	6.4
Once every 6 months	16	1.6
Once a year	51	5.0
At end of the contract	2	0.2
Other	0	0.0
Don't know	2	0.2
Total	1027	100.0
Source: SAMP Household Survey		

The "remittance package" of migrants from Lesotho also includes goods. Goods are purchased by migrants where they work and then sent or brought home to Lesotho. The proximity of the two countries makes this a feasible option, particularly since there is a greater range of consumer goods in South Africa and prices are generally lower. In addition, as members of a common customs union, there should be no duty to pay when migrants bring goods home. In practice, customs officials at official border posts do demand duty. MARS showed that 20% of migrant-sending households had received remittances in kind in the month prior to the survey. The average annual value of goods remitted to Lesotho was R2,487.

How do migrant-sending households compare with those that do not have migrant members? In another survey, SAMP collected data that compared income for migrant-sending households with a national sample of all households (Table 21).[78] Over half of the national sample (52%) reported an annual cash income of less than M2,500 compared to only 12% of migrant-sending households. Again, three quarters of the national sample have an income of less than M7,500 compared to 40% of the migrant-sending-households. In other words, while the vast majority of all households have very low incomes, the migrant-sending households are better off.

Table 21: Distribution of Household Income				
Household Income Group (M)	National Sample of Households		Migrant-Sending Households	
	%	Cumulative %	%	Cumulative %
0-2499	51.8	51.8	12.2	12.2
2,500-4,999	14.8	66.6	10.4	22.6
5,000-7,499	7.9	74.5	16.7	39.3
7,500-9,999	6.3	80.9	15.6	54.9
10,000-12,499	5.6	86.4	15.1	70.0
12,500-14,999	3.3	89.8	9.2	79.2
15,000-17,499	1.6	91.3	4.9	84.1
17,500-19,999	2.2	93.5	4.9	89.0
20,000-22,499	0.8	94.4	2.1	91.1
22,500-24,999	1.1	95.5	2.7	93.8
25,000-27,499	0.3	95.8	1.3	95.1
27,500-29,999	0.3	96.2	0.6	95.7
30,000-32,499	0.3	96.5	0.7	96.4
32,500-34,999	0.2	96.7	0.4	96.8
35000 and up	3.3	100.0	3.2	100.0
Source: SAMP Data Base				

REMITTANCE CHANNELS

The CDP system linking Lesotho with the South African mines is the primary formal channel for remittance flows. Outside the system, the most popular ways of remitting are informal. This is true for Lesotho and the region (Table 22). Migrants bring the money to Lesotho themselves (54%) or send it via a trusted friend or co-worker (33%). Very few use other formal money transfer systems; for example, only 5% use the Post Office and only 2% use banks. Easily the most popular way of sending goods home is to bring them personally (82%). A smaller number entrust them to friend or co-workers (12%). But only 4% use official rail transport channels and less than 1% entrust their goods to the taxis that ply the routes between Lesotho and the South African towns where they work.

Considerable attention is given in the remittance literature to the methods that migrants use to remit and the expense involved in remitting, through both formal and informal channels. The main policy recommendation is that governments and private sector institutions should lower the transaction costs of remitting, as well as make it easier for migrants to access and use formal channels through reform of banking and other financial regulations. In the case of Lesotho, hand-to-hand transfer of cash and goods is easily the most important channel. It is hard to see how transaction costs on personal transactions can be reduced unless the reason for return home is only to transfer remittances, in which case transportation costs make this a very costly means of remitting.

Table 22: Major Remittance Channels				
	Cash		Goods	
	Lesotho %	Region %	Lesotho %	Region %
Post Office	5.1	7.1	0.7	4.2
Wife's TEBA account	1.8	3.1	-	-
Bring personally	54.1	46.8	81.9	66.0
Via a friend/ co-worker	33.4	26.2	11.8	14.7
Via Bank in home country	1.8	6.1	-	-
Via TEBA own account	0.7	3.3	-	-
Bank in South Africa	0.9	0.8	-	-
Via Taxis	0.2	1.5	0.7	3.5
Bus	0.0	1.1	3.8	5.2
Rail	-	-	0.0	1.3
Other method	1.9	3.9	0.7	2.9
Total	100.0	100.0	100.0	100.0
Source: SAMP Household Survey				

Using friends and co-workers to carry cash and goods home is also relatively popular and, once again, quite feasible given geographical proximity. Problems that arise within this method pertain mainly to slowness and theft. Very few migrants cite either the cost of transactions or the lack of banking facilities as a problem for them. Basotho migrants do not generally see a problem in need of a solution. This does not mean that if cost-effective financial services were available, migrants would not use them. Some certainly might. But at the moment, most seem happier to take remittances with them when they go home.

The survey confirmed very low usage of formal institutions for money transfer between South Africa and Lesotho. The problem is not in moving money as both countries are members of the Rand Monetary Area (RMA). The Rand is legal tender in Lesotho (though not vice-versa). Many South African banks have branches in Lesotho but few migrants use the banks to remit. Generally, there is very low access to financial services in Lesotho.[79] Most migrants do not have bank accounts with the main banks and the costs of transfer, even within the RMA, are prohibitive. Bank products cost around R150 per transaction because banks charge a SWIFT fee and commission on each transaction even when funds are transferred to subsidiaries of the same bank in Lesotho.[80] A transfer to Maseru in Lesotho costs 700% more than a transfer to Ladybrand on the South African side of the border only kilometers away.[81] Undocumented Basotho migrants cannot open bank accounts in South Africa as a work permit is required to open a resident or non-resident account.[82]

Outside the CDP through Teba Bank, the Post Office is probably the most used formal channel (but only by 5% of migrants). The South African Post Office remits outside the country via money order or postal order but transaction costs are high (R30.50 for a R300 money order and R51.75 for a telegraphic money order).[83] Oganizations such as Western Union and MoneyGram do not operate in Lesotho. Less than 1% of migrants use TEBA Bank as their main method for transferring voluntary remittances. Slightly more (2%) pay remittances into spousal TEBA Bank accounts.

Informal Remitting

I am 42 years old and I have been a migrant for two years, when my husband became too sick to continue working on the South African mines. Before I stayed in Lesotho and looked after the household and children while my husband was away. We have four children: two are boys aged 21 and 16 and two girls 8 and 4. My oldest son has a high school education but could not find a job in Lesotho. He went last year to South Africa to work as an unskilled labourer. I think it is better for women to go to work in South Africa these days because every time you hear stories from men that there is no money, no work, or the job they were doing is finished.

I went because my husband was unable to work anymore and sitting together at home without a breadwinner made us reach a decision for me to go and fend for the family. I also wanted to earn some more money so that I could come back home and start some small business (a spaza shop). I heard about an employment agency north of Pretoria that was placing Basotho domestics with South African employers. So I went there and got a job.

I earn R12,000 a year. I send home R10,000 a year which is spent on food, clothing, fuel, hiring a tractor to plough the field and a small packet of seed to sow in my field. I post the money home or bring it myself after two months. This money is received by my husband. I do not make the decisions as to how the money I send is to be used. I send it to him because he is the one taking care of the children. I think this money makes a difference in providing food, for without it my children would die of hunger. One of my sons has to repeat Standard. He only got a third class pass but I do not know if the money I send will be enough to send him to school.

I want to save money but I am unable to do so. Even if I save, my [money] will not go towards my business. There are many deaths these days and the money saved would help in the burial of members of my household or me.

I have a Lesotho passport but I do not have a work permit. In order to remain in South Africa, I need to renew my visitor's permit once a month back at the border. I could overstay and then I have to pay a bribe of M150 to M200 demanded by officials at the border when I return to Lesotho.

Use of Remittances

Interviews with remittance senders and receivers suggest that the former decide how much to send and the latter make most of the decisions about how remittances will be spent. Although there are disagreements, very few respondents indicated that there is serious conflict about the use of remittances, probably because such a small proportion is ever truly discretionary. Once school fees are paid, health costs met, and clothing and groceries bought, there is not much left. Conflict arises when a spouse feels that the wage earner is wasting remittance money on non-essentials or is being dishonest:

> My husband is no use to our family at all and if things could be reversed it would be better if I went to work instead of him and maybe there would be some change in our lives. My husband does not send money and even when he brings it with him, he takes it to buy beer and entertain himself. He fights for it if I refuse to give him the money. When he comes home he does not even want to take a spade to dig the garden. He says he has come home to rest as he works hard in the mines. Him working in South Africa brings only negative impacts and he is no use at all to the family.[84]

Her spouse has been working for 20 years on the mines as a migrant. She had no idea how much he earns (but it is probably in excess of R30,000 a year). She claimed she only gets R3,000, all of which she spends on food and clothing, including for her niece and her husband's mother. The family, she said, do not have enough to eat many times during the course of the year. She is happy about compulsory deferred pay because she would otherwise "never see a cent of it." However, only her husband is able to withdraw the funds in Lesotho, which he does "without my knowledge and eats alone."

Both remitters and recipients agree that remittances are essential to the livelihood of household members and that without them they would be "lost." There are plenty of "lost" households in every village. The perceived importance of remittances proved to be extremely high (Table 23). Most households (89%) find the contribution of remittances to household income important or very important. Remittances are also key to having enough food in the household (with nearly 90% saying that it is important or very important).

Table 23: Perceived Importance of Remittances						
	Very Important	Important	Neutral	Not Important	Not Important at All	Don't Know
In Having Enough to Eat	73.4	16.5	2.2	3.0	4.7	0.2
In Having Enough Clean Water	40.2	17.3	9.6	11.6	20.8	0.6
In Accessing Medical Treatment	62.6	25.0	3.8	3.2	5.3	0.2
In Having Enough Cooking Fuel	58.7	28.5	3.9	2.2	6.5	0.2
In Having a Cash Income	63.1	25.7	2.9	2.5	5.6	0.1
N=1026						
Source: SAMP Household Survey						

How do migrant-sending households in Lesotho actually spend their remittance income? First, it is useful to look at household budgets (Table 24). Food and groceries are by far the most important expenditure (incurred by 93% of households in the month prior to the survey), followed by fuel (76%), clothes (73%), transportation (52%) and medical expenses (24%). Only 9% saved anything, 7% invested in farming and 5% spent on education. Over the course of a year, the proportion of households spending money on school fees would probably be much higher as all secondary school children in Lesotho have to pay fees at the beginning of the school year.

The average household spent M490 on food and M678 on clothes in the month prior to the survey. Much less was spent on the two other major items: fuel (M120) and transportation (M124). The households with medical expenses spent an average of M101. The 5% of households that spent on education incurred significant costs of M662. While only a small proportion of households had funds to spend on building, special events and farming, the average amounts were quite significant (M3,073, M2,176 and M642 respectively). Almost half (47%) of households had no savings. Less than 10% of households had saved any money in the previous month; those that did saved an average of M740. The largest monthly expenditure of all households combined was on clothes (29%), followed by food and groceries (27%), special events (9%), building (6%), fuel (5%), entertainment (4.2%) and transportation (2%).

Table 24: Monthly Household Expenses by Category				
	% of Households Incurring Expense	Average Amount Spent (M)	Total Amount Spent (M)	%
Food and groceries	92.5	490	462,560	26.9
Housing	0.9	150	1,350	0.0
Utilities	16.7	117	20,007	1.2
Clothes	72.7	673	499,366	29.0
Alcohol	12.0	209	25,707	1.5
Medical expenses	24.2	101	24,947	1.5
Transportation	52.3	124	71,556	2.4
Cigarettes, tobacco, snuff	10.5	84	8,968	0.5
Education	5.4	663	36,465	2.0
Entertainment	1.6	125	72,000	4.2
Savings	8.7	740	65,860	3.8
Fuel	76.3	120	93,480	5.4
Farming	7.1	642	46,224	2.7
Building	3.5	3,073	110,628	6.4
Special events	7.3	2,176	163,220	9.5
Gifts	3.6	119	4,403	0.3
Other expenses	1.2	1,060	12,720	0.7
Source: SAMP Household Survey				

The most common uses of remittances are for food (90% of households spent remittances on food), clothing (76%), school fees (56%) and fares for transportation (34%) (Table 25). In terms of agricultural inputs, a quarter of households spent remittances on seed, 18% on fertilizer, 12% on tractors and 4% on livestock. However, most of these agriculture-related expenditures were for subsistence food production. Nearly 19% of households put some remittance income into savings. Other expenditures such as funerals (incurred by 16% of households) and funeral and burial insurance policies (29%) reflect the impact of HIV/AIDS.

Table 25: Use of Remittances	
	% of HH
Food	89.3
Clothing	76.1
School fees	56.0
Fares	50.0
Funeral and burial policies	28.7
Seed	24.4
Savings	18.7
Fertiliser	18.5
Funeral	16.3
Tractor	12.5
Fuel	9.9
Feast	7.1
Cement	5.2
Labour	5.1
Bricks	4.5
Insurance policies	4.5
Doors and windows	3.8
Roofing	3.6
Dipping and veterinary costs	2.6
Oxen for ploughing	2.5
Other special events	2.2
Paint	2.0
Repay loans	1.9
Cattle purchase	1.4
Wood	1.3
Marriage	1.1
Purchase stock for sale	1.1
Small stock purchase	1.1
Poultry purchase	0.8
Vehicle purchase/maintenance	0.8
Vehicle and transport costs	0.6
Walls	0.7
Other farm input	0.4
Equipment	0.3
Labour costs	0.3
Machinery and equipment	0.1
Personal investment	0.0
Source: SAMP Household Survey	

The importance of basic needs expenditure is further highlighted when the estimated percentage of remittance money is examined for the most important expenditures (Table 26). For all major expense items the proportion of the remittance contribution is 80% and higher. Migrant-sending households in Lesotho thus spend the greater proportion of total income on basic necessities. In other words, consumption spending (for necessities, not luxuries) constitutes the predominant usage of household income, a pattern observed in many other parts of the developing world.

Table 26: Proportion of Expenses Paid from Remittances	
	%
Food and groceries	90.3
Housing	91.1
Utilities	85.1
Clothes	92.1
Alcohol	89.9
Medical expenses	86.4
Transportation	89.6
Cigarettes, tobacco, snuff	86.1
Education	86.8
Entertainment	100.0
Savings	83.0
Fuel	88.7
Farming	88.5
Building	91.2
Special events	85.4
Gifts	71.2
Total contributions from remittances	88.7
Source: SAMP Household Survey	

Further proof of the importance of migration to household food security and basic needs is seen in the types of goods that migrants sent home. There is little evidence of luxury goods being remitted. Instead, clothing (29% of households) and food (8%) are the items most frequently brought or sent (Table 27).

Remittance-receiving households are not the only ones to benefit from remittances. Within villages, there are formal and informal local relationships of obligation, reciprocity and charity with kin and neighbours by which remittances "spread" beyond the immediate beneficiary household. In most cases, remittances are spent on immediate household members, but are also passed on to other relatives, friends or poorer members of the community. One household, for example, consists of six people.[85] The de facto household head is a young male of 22, a university student. He looks after his younger brother (aged 18) and two younger sisters (aged 13 and 4). His two older sisters are both migrants to South Africa. One (aged 25) has been working in a shop in South Africa for 5 years. The other (aged 24) has just gone to South Africa for the first time. This household has four members in school yet receives no remittances at all directly from the two female migrant members in South Africa. Yet it still spent R4,000 on food, R1,700 on school fees and R1,500 on clothes over the previous year. The key is their widowed father. After their mother died, he moved in with a woman in another household. The two sisters send their remittances to their father "who decides how the money should be used." The father splits the money between his new household and that of his children.

Table 27: Proportion of Households Receiving Remitted Goods	
Type of Goods	%
Clothing	28.6
Food	7.6
Consumption Goods	2.5
Fuel	0.7
Equipment	0.5
Seed	0.2
Poultry	0.2
Goods for Funeral	0.2
Goods for Feast	0.2
Roofing	0.1

GENDER AND REMITTANCES

Four basic types of migrant-sending and remittance-receiving households were identified by MARS (Table 28):

- Female-headed: No husband/male partner; may include relatives, children, friends;
- Male-headed: No wife/female partner; may include relatives, children, friends;
- Nuclear: Man and woman with or without children; usually male-head;
- Extended: Man and woman and children and other relatives and non-relatives; male-head

The vast majority of male Basotho migrants (nearly 90%) come from nuclear and extended family households. Only 55% of female migrants come from such households. A significant minority (43%) come from female-headed households in which there is no husband or male partner (Table 28).

Table 28: Migrant-Sending Household Typology		
	Male Migrants	Female Migrants
Female-headed	7.0	42.9
Male-headed	3.8	0.7
Nuclear	43.3	18.6
Extended	45.9	37.8
Total	100	100
Source: SAMP Household Survey		

Most striking is the great significance of migrant remittances to household subsistence and basic material needs, regardless of migrant gender. The general importance of remittances is evident in the straightforward proportion of migrant-sending households that receive money from their migrant members (Table 29). At close to 90% in Lesotho, Swaziland and Zimbabwe, this is an extremely high figure in international comparative terms. Male migrants from Lesotho are slightly more likely to remit than female migrants. Given that male migrant labour is mainly in the mining sector, where remittances are compulsory, and that female migrant labour is in more precarious sectors of the South African labour market, it is surprising that this observed gender discrepancy in remittance behaviour is not higher.

Table 29: Proportion of Households Receiving Remittances		
Country	Male Migrant-Sending Households (%)	Female Migrant-Sending Households (%)
Lesotho	94.9	89.3
Mozambique	79.6	58.8
Swaziland	88.8	92.9
Zimbabwe	89.5	90.1
Source: SAMP Household Survey		

The amounts of money remitted by female migrants overall are significantly lower than those of male migrants (Table 30). Women's employment and livelihood strategies – for example as informal sector traders or domestic workers compared to waged mine labour – mean lower earnings overall and less regular or reliable remuneration. In addition, female migrants who are daughters, rather than spouses or heads of household, may remit a lower proportion of their earnings compared to male migrants, who are more likely to be heads of household and primary breadwinners.

Table 30: Average Annual Remittances Received from Male and Female Migrants		
	Male Migrants	Female Migrants
Mean	M11,162.46	M4,825.32
Median	M9,600.00	M3,600.00
Source: SAMP Household Survey		

While the gender differences in the monetary value of remittances are stark, Lesotho's female migrants remit significantly higher sums than their counterparts in Swaziland, Mozambique or Zimbabwe. This could be because the need for remittance income is greater in Lesotho, with fewer alternative livelihood options available and migrant-sending households being more directly dependent on migrant remittances. This is especially true for the female-headed households that make up a high proportion of Lesotho households sending female migrants.

Gender differences diminish significantly when remittances are considered in terms of their contribution to the household economy, rather than their absolute monetary value. Migrant remittances form an important, and in many cases the only, source of income for male and female migrant-sending households in Lesotho (Table 31). Over 95% of the households with male migrant members listed remittances as a source of household income. Fewer than 10% list income from the second-ranking income source, non-migrant wage labour. The equivalent proportions for female-sending households are around 90% and 15%. Households sending male migrants thus appear to be especially dependent on remittance earnings. This reflects both the higher proportion of male migrants who are household heads, and the higher earnings of male migrants, which make it more feasible to rely solely on remittances to meet basic household needs. Households sending female migrants are more likely to have to supplement remittance earnings with other sources of income, as female migrants remit lower sums. Female migrants are also less likely to be household heads, which means that they are often members of households with other working adult members, especially in cases where they come from extended families.

Taking these factors into consideration, it is again surprising that the gender discrepancies in remittance dependence are not greater. Lesotho's gender differences in household income sources are lower than for any of the other countries surveyed, including Zimbabwe. In sum, female migrant remittances are a demonstrably important source of both income and material goods for households sending female migrants. Whether they are household heads, spouses or daughters, women migrants are clearly sending significant sums of money and quantities of goods back to their families in Lesotho, contributing in no small way to those households' material welfare.

Table 31: Sources of Household Income in Male and Female Migrant-Sending Households		
Source of Household Income	Male Migrant-Sending (%)	Female Migrant-Sending (%)
Wage work	8.3	15.0
Casual work	5.0	12.1
Remittances – money	95.7	90.0
Remittances – goods	19.6	22.8
Farm product sales	2.4	2.8
Formal business	2.1	1.4
Informal business	6.5	6.4
Pension/ disability	0.2	2.1
Gifts	2.4	1.4
Other	0	0
Refused to answer	0	0
Don't know	0.5	2.1
N	841	140

Source: SAMP Household Survey
Note: Because many households had more than one source of income, percentages add up to more than 100%.

Female migrants and remittance recipients feel that their priorities in using remittances differ from those of men. As one Focus Group participant observed:

> Men and women spend money differently. Women often spend money inside the home while men on the other hand spend it outside the family. Men use the money to buy beer and other entertaining items while women would rather buy something that will benefit the whole family, such as buying food for the whole family. The man would take M100 of the money he brought home and use it to entertain himself alone but when he gets home he would demand food. The following day he takes another R100 and he would do that the whole holiday he is at home.[86]

Categories of household expenditure (Table 32) show only small differences between male and female migrant-sending households. What is different is the amount of money spent, which is considerably lower for households sending female migrants (Table 33).

Table 32: Proportion of Migrant-Sending Households Incurring Particular Expense

Expense Incurred in Previous Month	Male Migrant-Sending (%)	Female Migrant-Sending (%)
Food/Groceries	93.3	90.0
Housing	0.7	1.4
Utilities	17.7	12.1
Clothes	73.7	68.6
Alcohol	13.0	5.7
Medical costs	26.5	12.9
Transport	54.8	39.3
Tobacco	10.9	8.6
Education	5.7	3.6
Entertainment	1.7	0.7
Savings	10.1	2.1
Fuel	77.9	69.3
Farming	7.7	4.3
Building	3.9	0.7
Special events	7.7	5.7
Gifts	3.9	2.1
Other	0.8	1.4
N	841	140
Source: SAMP Household Survey		

Table 33: Migrant-Sending Household Expenditures[87]

Median Amount Spent in Previous Month (M)		
Category	Male Migrant-Sending (%)	Female Migrant-Sending (%)
Food/Groceries	400	215
Utilities	60	75
Clothes	500	350
Medical expenses	50	33
Transport	70	40
Education	230	230
Domestic fuel	90	50
Farming	350	100
Source: SAMP Household Survey		

The main household purchases for both male and female migrant-sending households are the basic commodities of food, domestic fuel, and clothing, in addition to fundamental services such as transport and health care (Table 32). In terms of the number of households reporting expenditure in a particular category in the previous month, the most common expenditures are, in rank order, food, domestic fuel (e.g. paraffin, wood, gas), clothing, and transport. Some gender differences emerge in the reported monetary expenditure in various categories (Table 33). Expenditure was found to be higher in almost every category for male compared to female migrant-sending households, and this was more consistently the case for Lesotho than for any of the other countries in the survey. This suggests that in Lesotho in particular, households with female migrant members (many of which, it should be recalled, were also female-headed) are indeed poorer and forced to 'go without' more often than households where the migrant members are men.

Given the weighting of overall household expenditures towards basic necessities, what is the role of remittances in enabling migrant-sending households to purchase certain goods and services? Are remittances spent on the same general basket of items? Or are they used for non-essential or luxury items, or perhaps directed towards savings or investment in business or other productive activities? Food is the most common annual expenditure of remittance earnings in both male- and female-migrant households (Table 34). Second is clothing, followed by school fees. Transport fares rank fourth, with funeral policies the fifth-greatest expenditure of remittance income.

Table 34: Ranking of Most Important Uses of Cash Remittances Over Previous Year	
Male Migrant-Sending Households	Female Migrant-Sending Households
Food	Food
Clothes	Clothes
Schooling	Schooling
Fares	Fares
Funeral policies	Funeral policies

Remittance-receiving households confirmed the significance of remittances to food purchases (Table 35). The most consistent importance rating, for both migrant genders, is food, with school fees and clothes also rated highly by many. There are some gender differences, with men's remittances seemingly more crucial to the purchase of basic livelihood items, such as food, than women's. Given that men are older, more likely to be married, and more often the heads of households than female migrants, it is perhaps surprising that this gender difference was not greater.

Table 35: Importance of Remittances in Annual Household Expenditure		Male Migrant-Sending (%)	Female Migrant-Sending (%)
Category		Male Migrant-Sending (%)	Female Migrant-Sending (%)
Food	Very important	72.0	68.6
	Important	8.0	8.6
Clothes	Very important	53.0	50.1
	Important	21.3	12.1
Schooling	Very important	50.8	37.9
	Important	8.0	8.6
Fares	Very important	39.0	80.0
	Important	13.3	7.9
Seed	Very important	20.7	27.1
	Important	4.5	1.4
Savings	Very important	16.4	27.1
	Important	4.5	5.7
Funeral policies	Very important	19.6	59.3
	Important	9.9	5.7
Funerals	Very important	9.5	40.7
	Important	6.8	7.1
N		841	140
Source: SAMP Household Survey			

What stands out is the fundamental importance of remittances in enabling migrant-sending households to meet their basic needs, such as food and clothing, and basic services such as transport and schooling. Remittances are used to some extent to support agricultural production through seed purchases but, given the low reported income from farm product sales, this is largely for household subsistence production. Categories in which households sending female migrants expressed higher importance of remittance income in meeting expenditure included transport, funerals and funeral policies, but otherwise the broad rankings are similar for male and female migrant-sending households. Remittance earnings certainly do not appear to be 'squandered' on luxury consumer items, but rather are used, either directly or indirectly, to meet the household's subsistence needs. In general, the pattern for expenditure of remittances reflects the patterns for overall household expenditure, and the households of both male and female migrants stressed the importance of remittances in enabling them to meet those needs.

The 'typical' male or female migrant from Lesotho sends home money, which their households use to buy food and other basic goods and services, and brings home clothing, food and consumer goods (Table 36). Consumer goods and 'luxury' items (e.g. electronic goods) are more readily available and also cheaper in South Africa, so it is not surprising to find them included here, but food and clothing still ranked well above consumer goods in stated importance. Again, there is a striking similarity between migrants of different gender.

Table 36: Most Important Goods Remitted by Migrants	
Male Migrant-Sending	Female Migrant-Sending
Clothes	Clothes
Food	Food
Consumer goods	Consumer goods

In addition to making regular remittances, migrants send money home in times of need or to meet unexpected costs. Funeral costs are by far the most common, along with funds for weddings and other feasts. Lesotho, which has the highest overall dependence on migrant remittances among the countries surveyed, reported the lowest incidence of such 'once-off' or emergency remittances, although the levels were still considerable. Some gender differences are evident (Table 37), with a higher proportion of male migrants reported as sending money in times of need. This may reflect their role as heads of household, with primary responsibility for meeting such emergency needs.

Table 37: Proportion of Households Receiving Emergency Remittances		
	Male Migrant-Sending (%)	Female Migrant-Sending (%)
Lesotho	44.0	37.1
Mozambique	59.3	35.3
Swaziland	51.9	61.9
Zimbabwe	54.8	54.2
Source: SAMP Household Survey		

Emergency remittances are clearly important to the households receiving them. They are seen as important or very important by 98% of migrant-sending households in Lesotho, with only very small differences on the basis of migrant gender (Table 38).

Table 38: Stated Importance of Emergency Remittances		
	Male Migrant-Sending (%)	Female Migrant-Sending (%)
Very important	73.9	70.6
Important	24.5	27.5
Source: SAMP Household Survey		

Overall, in gender terms, it is the similarities in the expenditure of remittances from male and female migrants that are so strong and revealing. Two important conclusions follow. First, for both male and female migrants, migration is commonly undertaken in the role of primary breadwinner, rather than as a supplement to other sources of household income. Second, remittances are more important as means of securing basic household livelihoods, alleviating poverty, and meeting emergency costs than as drivers of broader economic development.

Many Focus Group participants observed that it was increasingly common for migrant men to establish second households in South Africa. Sometimes these were relationships with South African women (in which case the migrant could acquire South African identity documents through marriage) and sometimes they were with migrant women from Lesotho. The losers, from the perspective of people in Lesotho, were their households at home:

> Most people we know, especially men, do have families in South Africa. In some cases they even leave with other women from Lesotho to live with in South Africa. The new family in South Africa puts a strain on the assistance the migrant brings to his original family in Lesotho. He now hardly ever sends or brings enough money to his Lesotho family, if at all.[88]

A female participant put it more bluntly: "Households that do not have migrants really struggle to make ends meet. But some also struggle as the husbands hardly ever send a cent home and this could be because they have families somewhere else."[89] Another felt that this phenomenon was causing more women to migrate:

> Women migrate in large numbers because our husbands can no longer be relied upon. Many of us still have husbands while the same number does not. I say men are unreliable because when they get to South Africa, they enter into extra-marital affairs and remarry. A man may actually leave home in the company of a local woman but sometimes he marries a South African woman. This implies that some Basotho women really go to look for jobs while others do not.[90]

The growing practice of establishing a new relationship, family or household in South Africa also has a clear gender dimension, according to respondents. Female migrants also have relationships with men in South Africa. In the case of male migrants, the practice leads to a decreased flow of remittances to the household in Lesotho. However, in the case of female migrants, it can actually augment rather than reduce the flow of remittances to Lesotho:

> Men often establish second families in South Africa so
> they have to share the money between two families. With
> women, on the other hand, even if they find boyfriends in
> South Africa they send the money the latter gives them
> home, together with the money they earn themselves.[91]

One woman noted cynically that most men in this position "forget about their original families" while women do not forget their families and children in Lesotho. A woman would rather take what her "men friends" give her and send it to her children.[92]

REMITTANCES AND POVERTY REDUCTION

Poverty continues to be the major driving force behind internal and cross-border migration in Lesotho. For most households (except the most skilled) migration remains a household survival strategy rather than a strategy for creating wealth and economic development opportunity. Several studies have mapped the pervasive nature of poverty in Lesotho, its causes and geographical distribution.[93] Two longitudinal studies of poverty in the 1990s showed that despite positive national economic growth (primarily from the Lesotho Highlands Water Project and the textile industry), poverty remained a chronic problem in Lesotho. One study compared data from National Household Budget Surveys in 1986-7 and 1994-5 and drew the following conclusion:

> The data show that the incidence and severity of poverty
> is greater among a number of social groups, female headed
> households, people living in rural areas, especially in the
> mountainous parts of Lesotho, the elderly, children, those
> who rely upon agricultural production and agricultural
> assets.[94]

The proportion of households below the poverty line was 58% at both points in time.[95] However, the severity of poverty increased for both poor and ultra-poor households. Poor households tended to be larger and with higher age dependency ratios. Other significant variables were the gender and employment status of the household head. In 1986-7, 27% of poor households were headed by women who were single, divorced, widowed or abandoned, a figure that rose to 30% in 1994-5. The proportion of female-headed households that were poor was 65% in 1986-7 and 62% in 1994-5 – a slight decrease. However, male-headed households in the poor category decreased from 65% to 58%. De facto female-headed households (those with a male migrant spouse) experienced an increase in the incidence and depth of poverty (from 48% to 55%), a clear consequence of lay-offs in the South African mining industry.

Unemployment was a key determinant of household poverty: more than two-thirds of households with an unemployed household head were below the poverty line at both points in time. Between 1986-7 and 1994-5, there was also a substantial increase in unemployment amongst heads of poor households (from 18% to 31%). The proportion of female-headed households falling below the poverty line increased from 70% to 78% during this time period. The other significant change was more positive: a fall in the proportion of households with self-employed heads falling below the poverty line from 67% to 42%. Marked changes also occurred in the major source of income for all households. In 1986-7, cash remittances were the major source of income for 35% of households, a figure that had dropped to 23% in 1994-5. Amongst the poor, the fall was 31% to 23% and amongst the non-poor, an even larger 40% to 24%. The proportion of households reporting local wages as the main source of income increased from 17% to 27% overall: from 23% to 42% for the non-poor and from only 13% to 16% for the poor. In other words, the relative importance of external versus internal wages as a source of household income shifted with mine retrenchments. And very few poor households were able to make that shift. The main fallback for poor households was agriculture (with 27% of households reporting it as the main source of income in 1986-7 and 42% in 1994-5).

Many of these trends are evident in another study that revisited 328 households in 2002 that were first interviewed in 1993.[96] The authors conclude that Lesotho's economic growth in the 1990s did not significantly reduce poverty. The proportion of poor households had risen to 68% by 2002. In 1993, 68% of the sample had no bank account or nothing in it; this had risen to 82% by 2002. Some 26% of the households were chronically poor (i.e. below the poverty line in 1993 and still there in 2002). Only 14% had risen above the poverty line while 28% had fallen below it (the "descending poor.").[97] A third of the descending poor households had experienced a change of head. Being chronically poor was also positively correlated with having a female head. Access to wage work (in Lesotho or in South Africa) was a critical determinant of whether households stayed above the poverty line. Those above or moving above had much more significant and consistent access than those that remained or fell below the poverty line. Some 34% of the households that had one or more wage workers in 1993 had none in 2002. Of these, 49% had declined into poverty.

The most recent snapshot of contemporary household poverty was provided by a 2006 SAMP poverty and migration survey of 1,224 households in all parts of Lesotho.[98] Of 3,197 household members over 18, only 22% were working full-time. Another 17% were working part-time, leaving 61% unemployed. The study used the Afrobarometer Lived

Poverty Index as a poverty measure.[99] The LPI shows that only 41% of households always have cash income and only 29% always have sufficient food (Table 39). As many as 23% said they never have enough food to eat. Asked to compare household economic circumstances with 12 months previously, 43% said they were worse and 11% much worse. Comparing households with and without migrants, the study found that 39% of migrant households but only 28% of non-migrant households satisfied their basic needs. As the study concludes: "There is a clear pattern from the data which suggests that households with migrant workers are more wealthy than those without and this clearly suggests that migration is a strong anti-poverty indicator." What is equally clear is that even households with part or full-time wage earners still struggle to secure a livelihood.

While remittances are essential to household subsistence and well-being, this does not give a sense of the gendered nature and intensity of the poverty and deprivation experienced by migrants' households. Female migrant-sending households in Lesotho are relatively more deprived than male migrant-sending households (Table 39). Slightly over half of female migrant-sending households reported going without food 'several times' or more in the previous year, compared to only 36% of male migrant-sending households. A similar pattern was found for deprivation from cash income: 62% for female migrant-sending households, 46% for male migrant-sending households. Deprivation indices were more gender-equivalent for electricity, water and fuel, but this is more a reflection of a general lack of service provision, especially in rural areas, than of poverty per se. Even for medicine and medical treatment, female migrant-sending households are worse off than male migrant-sending households.

Lesotho's female migrants (most of whom go to South Africa to work in domestic service) evidently come from very poor, severely deprived households that would likely be considerably worse off if they did not have migrant remittances as a source of income. That 'lived poverty' is so intensely and materially experienced by household members reinforces the finding that migration from Lesotho to South Africa is important as a household survival strategy.

In order to determine how the significance of migration is perceived by sending households, respondents were asked to assess its overall impact on a five-point scale from very positive to very negative. They were also asked questions about the most positive and most negative aspects of having household members working in another country. Respondents were broadly positive about the overall impact of migration, although more so for male than for female migration (Table 40). Close to 70% of the male migrant-sending household respondents in Lesotho regard migration as having positive or very positive impacts. The proportion for female migrant-sending households was lower at 59%.

Table 39: Frequency of Household Deprivation of Basic Needs in Previous Year		
	Male Migrant-Sending (%)	Female Migrant-Sending (%)
Gone Without Food		
Never	48.3	32.9
Once or twice	15.3	15.7
Several times	15.2	18.6
Many times	19.6	32.1
Always	1.5	0.7
Gone Without Clean Water		
Never	34.4	39.3
Once or twice	14.0	10.0
Several times	17.8	17.9
Many times	27.1	29.3
Always	6.7	3.6
Gone Without Medicine or Medical Treatment		
Never	37.6	32.1
Once or twice	28.2	25.7
Several times	18.3	20.7
Many times	14.3	17.9
Always	1.7	3.6
Gone Without Electricity		
Never	4.8	3.6
Once or twice	2.1	0.7
Several times	0.6	0.0
Many times	0.7	0.0
Always	91.8	95.7
Gone Without Fuel for Cooking		
Never	47.9	47.1
Once or twice	21.4	20.7
Several times	14.6	12.9
Many times	15.0	17.9
Always	1.1	1.4
Gone Without Cash Income		
Never	26.3	19.3
Once or twice	28.1	17.9
Several times	17.6	22.9
Many times	25.6	33.6
Always	2.4	5.7
Source: SAMP Household Survey		

Table 40: Perceived Overall Impact of Migration on the Household		
	Male Migrant-Sending (%)	Female Migrant-Sending (%)
Very positive	34.4	17.9
Positive	35.2	41.5
Neither	2.3	2.1
Negative	13.9	17.1
Very negative	12.7	20.7
Don't know	1.5	0.7
Total	100	100
N	841	140
Source: SAMP Household Survey		

A significant proportion of the female migrant-sending households from Lesotho regard the impact of migration as either negative or very negative (38% compared to 27% of the male migrant-sending households.) This is especially interesting given the high levels of poverty and deprivation in Lesotho's female migrant-sending households and the significant contribution made by female migrant remittances to household income and expenditure. Possible explanations are that the social costs of migration are felt to outweigh the economic gains; or alternatively, that female migration is indeed a 'last resort', and thus a source of shame and embarrassment to the household, especially if it is related to marital breakdown or to perceived male failure to earn a living for the family. Female migration itself may be regarded by many in Lesotho as socially inappropriate or undesirable, even though it is recognized as economically necessary.

Perceptions of the positive impacts of working in another country reinforce the findings from income, expenditure and deprivation data, i.e. that migration primarily improves household livelihoods (Table 41). Differences based on the gender of the migrant are small. This supports the finding that female migration is as economically important as male migration, at least to the migrant-sending households themselves.

Table 41: Most Positive Effects of Migration on the Household		
	Male Migrant-Sending (%)	Female Migrant-Sending (%)
None	16.2	24.7
Supports household	6.9	5.6
Improved living conditions	63.2	58.6
Supports children's education	11.7	11.1
Job opportunities	<1	0.0
Migrant acquires skills	<1	0.0
N	841	140
Source: SAMP Household Survey		

Most Basotho families are simply struggling to survive. Remittances are directed almost exclusively to the basic needs of household members. The bulk of remittances are spent on necessities such as food, clothing, school fees, medical supplies, cooking fuel and transportation. Very little is left over for investment in agricultural production or small business development. Savings are almost non-existent. Yet, in some ways, the country's migrant-sending households are actually the fortunate few. They are not at the top of the economic ladder, but they are above the great majority at the bottom.

REMITTANCES AND AGRICULTURE

Lesotho is still a predominantly rural society although urbanization is proceeding very rapidly. One reason, among many, is declining agricultural production and productivity. Cereal production reached a high of about 200 kg per person in the mid-1970s but is currently around the 50-60 kg level. The expected figure for the 2007 season was its lowest point ever at 40 kg per person. The FAO standard for subsistence production of cereal crops is a minimum of 180 kg per person, so that at present Lesotho is producing less than a quarter of expected needs. Food insecurity is a constant for many households. Every year, large quantities of the primary staple, maize, are imported from South Africa.[100] Given the grave lack of employment, the World Food Programme declared a serious emergency in 2007-8 when about 400,000 people faced severe food insecurity.

Much of the recent difficulty can be attributed to drought, with severe weather conditions prevailing over much of Southern Africa during the period between 2004 and 2007. But loss of soil fertility is another factor, since Lesotho's arable land has been over-cultivated for many years. A further reason is a slow reduction over the years in the number of fields being cultivated. The downsizing of the mine migrant labour system has reinforced the marginal position of farming in Lesotho. Households without access to mine remittances no longer have the resources to invest in agriculture. Another factor of increasing importance is the loss of able-bodied agricultural labour because of HIV and AIDS. Many fields are still cultivated, but the challenge is enormous: "Those affected households that struggle on, often headed by old people or orphans, typically suffer poverty because they are no longer able to farm as they did before, and/or because their capacity to generate off-farm income has dwindled or disappeared."[101]

MARS provided new insights into the relationship between agriculture and remittances (Table 42). Around a quarter of households bought seed and one in five bought fertilizer. Around 15 percent used remittances to assist with ploughing. Five percent used remittances to employ people in their fields but less than 2% used remittances to purchase cattle. In other words, almost three-quarters of households do not spend any of their remittances on agriculture-related activity. The survey also showed that less than 3% of households receive income from the sale of farm products. In other words, even when remittances are invested in agriculture this is largely to try to increase food production for own consumption.

Table 42: Use of Remittances for Agriculture	
	% of HH
Seed	24.4
Fertiliser	18.5
Tractor Hire	12.5
Oxen for ploughing	2.5
Labour	5.1
Cattle purchase	1.4
Small stock purchase	1.1
Poultry purchase	0.8
Dipping and veterinary costs	2.6
Vehicle and transport costs	0.6
Equipment	0.3
Other farm input	0.4
Source: SAMP Household Survey	

The experience of one ex-migrant farmer, a man of 70, clearly illustrates the constraints that households face.[102] Many households have no land which means they are unable to farm at all. This particular man does have fields. His daughter and son are both migrants but he finds the former a far more reliable remitter perhaps, he says, because he is looking after her 13-year old son. However, she only remits R800 a year. He uses the money to hire casual workers from the village to help him plough and plant. He grows maize and wheat and sells his surplus produce and earns about R1,600 a year. Most of this is spent on purchasing food and groceries so that he and his granddaughter and another young man who lives with him can have a more varied diet.

His main challenges as a farmer are "the weather conditions, the worst enemy being the droughts and hail, the other one is the attack of the plants by pests" and lack of government support. He would like help with a threshing machine, a place to store grain and a place to buy seeds and insecticides. He has considered cash cropping of vegetables, "but the problem is theft." Another respondent said he receives the R3,000 remitted by his working spouse in a similar manner, although he only grows sorghum which he either sells "as is" or turns into malt which he sells to beer-brewers in the area. His income from the sale of produce was R3,500 the previous year. What is interesting about these two cases is that they are both older men who view themselves as farmers and say they have been farming since their youth. Few of today's young men and women would describe themselves this way.

Minding the Store

I am 48 years old. My husband has worked for many years on the mines. I do not know how much he earns but I receive about R17,000. The money is spent on food, transport, fuel, my mother-in-law's monthly hospital visits and paying school fees for my brother-in-law's three children who live in another household. The money is also used to cover the farming activities like purchase of seed and fertilizer and paying for help with ploughing, planting and harvesting. We grow food for our own use. Without the money from my husband, these activities would not be possible. We would surely struggle to make ends meet.

We agreed that I should start a business using the money. I chose to open a shop because it is the only kind of business I can operate myself although I sometimes hire someone to help out. I am responsible for manning the shop, being a shop clerk. I draw lists of stocks that need replenishing and go to Maseru (the capital city) myself to buy the stocks. I also do the pricing of items and the cleaning of the premises. The business is now successful as it is self-sustaining and no longer depends on outside sources of money to survive. The worst problem I experienced was that I gave things to fellow villagers on credit and they delayed paying me, while some even failed paying at all. My business collapsed and my husband came to the rescue and injected remittance money. Now I no longer give credit.

We have purchased several minibus taxis with his remittance money. However, this business was not very successful with him away and now we are left with only one taxi, which we pay someone to operate.

I make about R24,000 profit a year from the shop but the competition is closing in and it is non-Basotho. I feel angry about the foreign business owners, especially the Chinese, who are renting shops even at the village level and undercutting my prices. As a result, no one goes to Basotho-owned shops any longer.

REMITTANCES AND SMALL BUSINESS DEVELOPMENT

The proportion of migrant-sending households investing remittances in formal and informal business is extremely low in Lesotho. There is also no statistically significant difference between male and female migrant-sending households. This is an important point as households with male migrants receive more in remittances than households with female migrants. Yet, the overwhelming majority of households in both categories (over 90%) do not receive income from the sale of farm produce or from formal or informal business. And even the very small minority who do make extra income from these sources do not make large sums (an average of R6,708 p.a. in formal business, R3,066 p.a. in the informal sector and only R1,526 p.a. from the sale of farm produce) (Table 43).

Table 43: Sources of Household Income in Male and Female Migrant-Sending Households			
Source of Household Income	Male Migrant-Sending (%)	Female Migrant-Sending (%)	Average Income (M)
Farm product sales	2.4	2.8	1,525.93
Formal business	2.1	1.4	6,708.00
Informal business	6.5	6.4	3,066.41
N	841	140	
Source: SAMP Household Survey			

Remittances to Lesotho are largely a zero-sum game. The money comes in from South Africa and is spent mostly on South African or other foreign imports, especially foodstuffs and clothing. Efforts to create small businesses through sharing of resources have not been successful over the years. CARE attempted in the 1980s and 1990s to create mohair-spinning and seed-multiplication projects. They depended on foreign subsidies to keep going, and in the end only one made even a marginal impact on the economy of the village where it was located. IFAD developed credit associations in roughly the same time period, but they never succeeded. The Ministry of Agriculture's credit union was useful only to provide seed to farmers, but it always lost money, mostly because of bad loans.

The qualitative research identified a few individuals who did use remittances for some form of entrepreneurial activity. Their experience is certainly of relevance since it (a) helps explain why so few households in Lesotho invest remittances in entrepreneurial activity; (b) identifies the obstacles which entrepreneurial individuals face and (c) permits recommendations on how the proportion of entrepreneurs might be expanded.

One young skilled manual worker in the construction industry in

Johannesburg has worked for a building contractor for two years.[103] He is an irregular migrant and earns R22,000 a year. He remits around R5,000 a year in cash and R7,000 worth of goods to his large household:

> I am the main provider in the household of twelve people. All these people need food and clothing. The money I send meets only two basic needs i.e. food and soap. There are complaints about the amount of money I send because they are a large family. I normally send the money to my two older brothers who are in charge. We have one married sister working in South Africa as well. I send the money home through the bank. Owing to the size of the household, the money is just enough to buy food, but little as it is it makes some difference because without it, life would be difficult. When anybody falls ill at home, they just phone me and I send the money as they require.

The sheer size of the household places an extraordinary burden. However, he believes that there are "business opportunities for citizens of Lesotho (in South Africa) but the problem is getting proper documentation and raising enough funds." His aim is certainly "to open a business thus helping my family and community." He has begun in a small way and made R800 in December: "When I am here at this time of year, I sell beer, soft drinks and some cigarettes. The business is doing well particularly at this time of year. When I go back to South Africa, I think it will die a natural death unless my other brothers who are still here give it a serious thought."

Several female entrepreneurs have realized the 'dream' of opening small shops though not without considerable obstacles. All are married to current or ex-miners and have successfully used mine remittances in their small business ventures. Perhaps the most successful is in her mid-40s and lives with her teenage daughter and 24-year old son.[104] Her spouse has been working on the mines for 18 years and currently remits around R36,000 p.a. She started a grocery shop with remittances but did not generate much profit. In 2008, she switched to selling alcohol that she buys from a liquor store in another village. She hires someone to run the store and made a profit of R92,400 in 2008. Of this she saved R24,000 p.a. at a bank as a retirement fund for her and her husband. Her plans for further expansion are hampered only by her inability to get a substantial loan. Another successful entrepreneur is a 25-year-old who supports her elderly mother and four children.[105] When her husband was retrenched from the mines, she started a small spaza shop brewing and selling traditional beer and buying and selling small items such as matches and candles. Her husband got another job in South Africa and continues to remit about R10,000 p.a. She travels to the capital Maseru to buy goods for her shop where she also sells vegetables she has grown at home. She makes about R3,000 a year from the shop and another R1,500 from beer sales. Her transport costs to and from Maseru are exorbitant (R2,500 a year). In the villages, there is also increasing competition from Chinese storeowners.

Individual entrepreneurial opportunities in the rural villages are limited. Though not everyone can run or afford to run a spaza or a sheebeen, many of these outlets throughout the country were started (and are sometimes sustained) by remittances. However, the start-up and running costs (even with low overheads) are such that these are run primarily by the spouses of migrant mineworkers (who are amongst the best-paid migrants).

Focus Group participants spoke of current and ex-mineworkers who have also successfully entered the taxi business. One man had started by running a shop and then bought a minibus taxi with the proceeds: "Now he has many."[106] Another man got together with his friends from another village and started a taxi business. He first purchased a second-hand taxi and then worked "very hard" until he was able to buy another. He now owns five and hires drivers and conductors. Public transport is poor in Lesotho and many people travel by minibus taxi within the country and when they go to South Africa. The routes are highly competitive and it is a cut-throat business. The capital outlay is considerable, however, and well beyond the means of most migrant workers, especially women.

In the villages in Lesotho, burial societies and grocery associations effectively "pool" a portion of remittance receipts though not primarily for entrepreneurial reasons. Two Focus Group respondents described how these operate:

> There are burial societies within the community and members have to pay monthly contributions towards the time when one of the members has a death in the family and the society has to pay what is due to them. There are also grocery associations whereby monthly payments are also made by members towards purchasing of Christmas groceries and food. The money is also available for borrowing by members, to be paid back with interest. The main problem is non-payment of borrowed money and interest. There are separate male and female associations within the community. The women have the grocery associations.[107]

> There are associations within the community. There are burial societies and an egg producer association known as Egg Circle, where members are given the privilege of having

their eggs sold before everyone else. Burial societies differ but members commonly pay a monthly subscription of an agreed amount and when they have a death in the family the society gives them their agreed dues, whether money, a coffin or a cow. Problems occur when people do not pay their subscription for a long time in which case they would receive nothing if they had a death, unless they pay what they owe. The other problem is that more people are dying from AIDS these days and that puts strain on the coffers of the societies as sometimes the societies would have as many as three deaths in a week or month whereas before they would sometimes spend as long as six months without a death.[108]

Respondents in one village said there were a lot of "women's organizations" in the area including food and grocery associations. As well as loaning out money to be paid back with interest at the end of the year, the associations buy food and groceries in bulk to divide among themselves. There is also a men's-only association but the women are "leaving them in the dust" as their associations are growing "in leaps and bounds."[109]

The household survey showed that 12% of households borrowed money from informal moneylenders in the previous year. Some of the moneylenders are actually migrants who use their earnings (in South Africa) and remittances (in Lesotho) to loan money to needy persons or households. While it is a useful way for the benefits of remittances to be spread more broadly, most households only borrow to meet emergencies. Informal moneylenders are known as *bo-machonisa* (loan sharks) in Lesotho and charge their clients "inhumane" interest.[110] They commonly take people's passports as surety for loans and charge interest rates of 30-50%. One mineworker interviewed for this study, for example, joined with a group of friends and they all pay R2,000 into a common pool at the beginning of each year. They then make loans to those who need emergency funds and charge interest of 50%. At the end of the year, they receive their original investment back plus their share of the profits. According to the migrant, this helps him to cover the extra costs of the 'festive season.' Such enterprising activity is viewed with distaste by poorer households or those who are forced for lack of alternatives to avail themselves of the moneylending 'service.' This form of 'entrepreneurship' may be a profitable use of remittances but it clearly undermines social capital and deepens the poverty of other households.

The main obstacle that confronts many migrants and remittance-receiving households is the small size of the remittance package and the fact that most of it is consumed on daily expenses. Most households find that by the time the remittance package has been spent on basic needs (food, clothing, transport, fuel, school fees and hospital visits), there is very little left over for productive income-generating investment. There is a clear gender dimension to this issue. As noted above, men (mainly migrant miners) can earn three or four times as much as women (mainly domestic and farm workers) and can remit more than women. Women's earnings and remittances are paltry and the researchers were able to find only one household where women's remittances were used (in this case by their father) to generate additional income through farming. However, the household was small and the expenditures on basic needs lower so there was a small surplus. Focus Group respondents were keen to explain how difficult it is in Lesotho to use remittances to establish a business. As one man noted:

> It is not easy to establish some business. Let me explain it this way. I may send money home but it happens that it is not enough for a business because, first, when I left, I might already have had some debts....There is also too much sharing of money before it reaches the destination. It is TEBA this side, debts on the other and clothing for the children there, so it cannot be used for business. There is no migrant who has managed to establish a business here.[111]

The female migrants concurred: "Money that we send home is not used for farming nor for business." The money is "all used for family needs and there is always none left to start a business."[112] The fact that so few households in the national survey invest in business activity certainly bears this out.

One woman stated quite categorically that, "remittances are not used for business purposes, whether big or small. Money is often sent to cover certain needs. The money that is sent is little and after all is done, nothing remains to start a business."[113] In many cases, migrants remit whatever they can and there is little or any surplus at the end of the month to save, invest, or to establish a small enterprise. However, the proportion of the wage package that is remitted does vary considerably even amongst migrants making the same amount of money.

Part of this is because of the variable costs that migrants encounter in South Africa. Migrant miners and most domestic workers usually get free board and lodging while at work. Others have to pay rent and for their own food. If the migrant is in another relationship or has a second household in South Africa, the remittance flow to Lesotho is reduced accordingly. However, it is still likely that there is an element of discretion in voluntary remitting. In other words, it is possible that the amount remitted is actually determined by the livelihood needs of the household and that any surplus remains in South Africa and is spent there. Why, in other words, send more when there are so few opportunities for business development in Lesotho?

The second major obstacle is the lack of capital and loan financing for those who wish to develop a business. Some respondents blamed the government for not assisting more:

> You come with the little you worked for with difficulty but you will be required to pay for so many things that what you had will get finished even before you start. When you establish a business your intention is to live and help other Basotho do so but our government does not help. There is a boulder blocking and we are not aware of it.[114]

Others complained about the lack of loan facilities: "Our banks, which have our money, cannot give us loans."[115] Even micro-finance is difficult to obtain in Lesotho.

Most migrant-sending households are forced to borrow money during the course of the year, because the remittance flow is either insufficient or irregular (Table 44). The majority (46%) borrow from family and friends, presumably largely interest-free. Very few borrow to finance an entrepreneurial activity. Less than 1% had borrowed money from banks or formal moneylenders. Less than 5% had obtained loans from micro-finance organizations. Apart from family and friends, the most common way of obtaining a loan was from informal moneylenders (12% of households).

Table 44: Sources of Borrowed Funds	
	%
Friends	28.0
Employer	0.5
Burial society	5.9
Family	18.3
Church	0.2
Bank	0.4
Savings group	3.4
Union	2.9
Moneylenders (formal)	0.5
Moneylenders (informal)	12.1
Micro-finance organisations	4.3
Other source	0.1
Source: SAMP Household Survey	

Thirdly, the net worth of remittance transfers is reduced in several ways. As noted, there are the transaction costs of money transfer. Very few migrants use formal money transfer channels so this is not as big an issue as it is in other countries. However, transaction costs are not absent even for informal channels. Net income, and therefore remitting potential, is also reduced by the fact that some migrants are double-taxed (in South Africa and again in Lesotho). Then there is the major problem of corruption. Some miners were particularly critical of their recruiting agency, TEBA, and its Lesotho operations:

> We normally send money home through TEBA but the problem is our spouses have to stand in long queues and sometimes end up not receiving the money. There is much corruption at TEBA. Our spouses are forced to pay bribes to get the service. It is painful that you remit M1,000 and M20 is deducted for a bribe. The money now is already short to cover all that was supposed to be covered. TEBA does not care for us mineworkers.[116]

No doubt this kind of corruption by TEBA employees is not condoned by management but they could do more to root it out. Also problematic for migrants is widespread corruption at the border. One study even argues that border posts between South Africa exist not to control the flow of people but to allow the personal enrichment of border officials.[117] Again, this "business of the border" is not condoned by either government but they seem powerless to prevent it. One of the major forms of corruption that emerged in this study was the practice of permit renewal forced on migrants by the fact that entry to South Africa is limited to 30 days. Migrants who have overstayed in South Africa have to pay bribes to border officials on return or, alternatively, pay for their passports to be taken to the border for stamping, and thus more money flows into official pockets.

Fourthly, the surveys discussed in this report indicate that remitting from South Africa takes the following form: a migrant from a household goes to South Africa, works and remits small amounts at regular intervals to the individual household who spend the funds on basic needs such as food, clothing, education, health and transport. There is no evidence of what has been called in other contexts "collective remitting"; that is, groups of migrants pooling remittances and remitting to support a broader community development initiative. But migrants do form mutual help associations in South Africa (such as stokvels and burial societies) and in Lesotho itself there are mutual help associations in virtually every village and community (burial societies, grocery associations and egg circles). Further research is needed on the operation, organization and impact of these associations. They are grassroots organizations amongst migrant-sending households and help to build social capital in migrant communities. Their potential as development agents has barely been examined but it seems that they do have considerable potential, if supported in the right way, to add development value to the efforts of individual migrants at the level of the community as a whole.

A fifth obstacle to improving the development impacts of migration and remittances is inherent to the regulatory framework governing movement between Lesotho and South Africa. Only miners and some skilled migrants can get residence and work permits in South Africa. Everyone else has to go on 30-day visitor's permits. The moment they work in South Africa they are doing so irregularly. This makes migrants vulnerable to exploitation by employers, compromises their basic rights and means that they cannot do simple things like open a bank account in South Africa. Lesotho places no restrictions on the migration of its citizens to South Africa for work. The government's only concern is that people do not move permanently to South Africa or cut their ties with home. This concern is founded on the fear that scarce skills will be lost and remittance flows will decline.

Finally, a major obstacle to realizing the development potential of remittances in Lesotho lies in "structural development constraints":

> A critical reading of the empirical literature leads to the conclusion that it would be naïve to think that despite their often considerable benefits for individuals and communities, migration and remittances alone can remove more structural development constraints. Despite their development potential, migrants and remittances can neither be blamed for a lack of development nor be expected to trigger take-off development in generally unattractive investment environments. By increasing selectivity and suffering among migrants, current immigration restrictions have a negative impact on migrants' wellbeing as well as the poverty and inequality.[118]

There can be few peaceful developing countries where the "investment environment" is more unattractive than in Lesotho. In other words, even if receiving households had remittances to invest in entrepreneurial and other income-generating activities, what could they possibly invest in? This raises a key issue that requires further exploration. How feasible is it for migrant workers from Lesotho to engage in entrepreneurial activities in South Africa where the opportunities are much greater than in Lesotho? Can loans and micro-credit be obtained more easily in South Africa? These questions suggest that it is important to stop seeing

Lesotho as the only site for entrepreneurship by migrants from Lesotho. South Africa should also be seen as a potential site and market for the migrant entrepreneur and his or her dependents. Certainly this is very true for cross-border traders who buy and sell in South African towns. It should also be true for other forms of business enterprise. This would require a change in public policy in South Africa.

Policy Implications

There is little doubt that South Africa would never have developed into a modern industrial state without cheap migrant labour from neighbouring countries such as Lesotho. If Lesotho were ever to claim reparations for the value of labour expended and lives lost and families wrecked by the South African mines, the claim would probably bankrupt the South African fiscus. We make this point only to indicate that the development of South Africa and Lesotho are inextricably linked, and always have been: "If Lesotho and South Africa were truly distinct and separate, it would be natural to speak of migration or immigration" from one to the other.[119] But they are not.

Lesotho is an impoverished, dependent and economically vulnerable state because of South Africa. Basotho migrants cannot be kept out of South Africa and they will come in ever greater numbers if the only employment and other economic opportunities are in South Africa itself. That much is certain. But why should South African employers be permitted to take advantage of their poverty and vulnerable status by paying them sub-minimum wages, abusing their basic labour and human rights and using them to undercut unions and undermine labour standards? Lesotho ratified the UN ICMW in the hope that South Africa would do likewise and begin to offer its migrants basic rights and protections, not a continuation of the situation under apartheid.[120] So far, the South African government (like receiving states around the world) has studiously ignored the Convention.

Migration needs to be re-conceptualized in public policy not as a threat to the interests of South Africans but as something that is (and could be even more) mutually beneficial to both countries. The only realistic way for this to happen is to open the border to free travel in both directions. This would involve allowing Basotho to own land and seek jobs in South Africa without losing their citizenship. Lesotho's government would continue to be responsible for social services within its own borders, but Basotho would have the chance to improve their material conditions within South Africa and to remit in much greater volumes to their dependants that remain at home.[121]

The SADC Protocol on the Facilitation of Movement has been formally adopted at the Summit of the Heads of States and been signed by nine member states which now allows for the drafting of an implementation plan.[122] However, for the Protocol to come into effect, at least nine member states must have ratified it. The ultimate objective of the protocol is "is to develop policies aimed at the progressive elimination of obstacles to the movement of persons of the Region generally into and within the territories of State Parties" by facilitating three types of movement:

- Entry, for a lawful purpose and without a visa, into the territory of another State for a maximum period of ninety (90) days per year for bona fide visits and in accordance with the laws of the State concerned. The person must enter through an official border post, possess valid travel documents and produce evidence of sufficient means of support for the duration of the visit. The Protocol is silent on what a migrant may or may not do during these three months.
- Movement for Residence defined as "permission or authority, to live in the territory of a State Party in accordance with the legislative and administrative provisions of that State Party." The Protocol also encourages member states to facilitate the issuing of residence permits;
- Movement known as Establishment defined as "permission or authority granted by a State Party in terms of its national laws, to a citizen of another State Party, for: (a) exercise of economic activity and profession either as an employee or a self-employed person; and (b) establishing and managing a profession, trade, business or calling.

The Protocol makes it clear that entry for all three reasons will be governed by the national legislation of the SADC member state that they are entering.

In 2001, the Departments of Home Affairs in both South Africa and Lesotho asked SAMP to conduct research on cross-border movement between the two countries and to make recommendations on how to facilitate movement between them. This resulted in an extensive report that questioned whether the considerable resources to manage border operations were being effectively utilized and recommended the downgrading of the current border regime.[123] A Joint Bilateral Commission for Co-operation (JBCC) between the two countries was signed in 2001. The JBCC is used as a vehicle to drive forward areas of co-operation between the two countries and by mid-2007, 20 subsidiary cooperation agreements had been signed.

Since Lesotho and South Africa have both ratified the Protocol, they clearly have no fundamental objections. There is therefore every reason for them to move forward bilaterally to implement all three phases with immediate effect. In 2002, a bilateral Agreement on the Facilitation of Cross Border Movement of Citizens between South Africa and Lesotho was drafted. The Agreement was independently approved by the Cabinets of both countries in 2005-6 and finally signed in June 2007. This agreement calls primarily for an easing of border controls between the two countries. This is a start but it does not go nearly far enough and has still not been implemented. The aim of both states should be a broader agreement which is consistent with the SADC Protocol and which includes not only Entry but also Residence and, especially, Establishment.

The research for this report has shown, at the national and household level, that migration from Lesotho is deeply and profoundly gendered. Feminization of migration is proceeding rapidly but this does not mean that a homogenous de-gendered "migrant" is emerging. There are major and entrenched differences between male and female migrants in terms of their socio-demographic profile, their occupations and opportunities in South Africa and their remitting behavior. Similarly, within Lesotho itself, there are significant differences between male-sending and female-sending households. The latter are worse off than the former and have even fewer opportunities for income-generating activity outside of migration. The gendered nature of migration and its differential impact on men and women needs to be recognized and factored into all debates and policies for mainstreaming migration in development in Lesotho.

The migration and development debate has been hampered by the fact that the main "players" are nation-states between which migrants move or circulate. This is particularly problematic in the case of South Africa and Lesotho because it foregrounds the role of regulatory frameworks and control policies in relation to migration between the two countries. As this report has argued, it is precisely this kind of thinking that has seriously hampered two states that are inextricably bound together in every way from moving forward to a 'new immigration compact' of free movement, unrestricted economic opportunity and heightened remittance flow. There are promising signs that the reality of co-development is being recognized but much more needs to be done to ensure that the migration and remittance regime becomes a true "win-win" for both countries and for both male and female migrants.

ENDNOTES

1   World Bank, *Migration and Remittances Factbook: 2008* (Washington: World Bank, 2008).

2   UNDP-Lesotho, *Lesotho National Human Development Report 2006* (Morija: Morija Printing Works, 2007), p. 10.

3   C. Van der Wiel, *Migratory Wage Labour: Its Role in the Economy of Lesotho* (Mazenod: Mazenod Publishing, 1977); A. Spiegel, "Migrant Labour Remittances, the Developmental Cycle and Rural Differentiation in a Lesotho Community" M.A. Thesis, University of Cape Town, 1979; A. Spiegel, "Rural Differentiation and the Diffusion of Migrant Labour Remittances in Lesotho," In P. Mayer, ed., *Black Villagers in an Industrial Society: Anthropological Perspectives on Labour Migration in Southern Africa* (Cape Town: Oxford University Press, 1980); C. Murray, *Families Divided: The Impact of Migrant Labour in Lesotho* (Cambridge: Cambridge University Press, 1981); J. Cobbe, "Emigration and Development in Southern Africa, With Special Reference to Lesotho" *International Migration Review* 16 (4) (1982): 37-68; J. Crush and O. Namasasu, "Rural Rehabilitation in the Basotho Labour Reserve" *Applied Geography* 5 (1985): 83-98.

4   See S. Maimbo and D. Ratha, eds., *Remittances: Development Impacts and Future Prospects* (Washington DC: World Bank, 2005); World Bank, *Global Economic Prospects: Economic Implications of Remittances and Migration* (Washington: World Bank, 2005); C. Ozden and M. Schiff, eds., *International Migration, Remittances and the Brain Drain* (Washington DC: World Bank, 2006).

5   B. Roberts, *A Migration Audit of Poverty Reduction Strategies in Southern Africa* MIDSA Report No. 3, SAMP, Cape Town, 2005, p. 33.

6   UNDP-Lesotho, *Lesotho National Human Development Report 2006*, pp. 10, 33.

7   J. Crush, "Migration and Development in Southern Africa" Report for International Labour Organization, Geneva, 2007.

8   See http://www.queensu.ca/samp/midsa

9   Commonwealth Secretariat, "Report on a Workshop on Foreign Remittances and Development in the SADC Region" Maseru, 2006.

10 Murray, *Families Divided*.

11 J. Cobbe, "Approaches to Conceptualization and Measurement of the Social Cost of Labour Migration from Lesotho" In Agency for Industrial Mission, *South Africa Today: A Good Host Country for Migrant Workers?* (Johannesburg: AIM, 1976); J. Cobbe, "Emigration and Development in Southern Africa, With Special Reference to Lesotho" *International Migration Review* 16 (4) (1982): 37-68; Murray, *Families Divided*; J. Gay, "Basotho Women Migrants: A Case Study" *Institute of Development Studies Bulletin* 11(3) (1980): 19-28; J. Gay, "Wage Employment of Rural Basotho Women: A Case Study" *South African Labour Bulletin* 6(4) (1980): 40-53; Spiegel, "Migrant Labour

Remittances"; Spiegel, "Rural Differentiation"; E. Gordon, "An Analysis of the Impact of Labour Migration on the Lives of Women in Lesotho" *Journal of Development Studies* 17 (3) (1981): 59-76; J. Bardill and J. Cobbe, *Lesotho: Dilemmas of Dependence in Southern Africa* (Boulder: Westview Press, 1985); J. Plath, D. Holland and D. Carvalho, "Labour Migration in Southern Africa and Agricultural Development: Some Lessons from Lesotho" *Journal of Developing Areas* 21 (1) (1987): 159-75; R. Wilkinson, "Migration in Lesotho: A Study of Population Movement in a Labour Reserve Economy" PhD Thesis, University of Newcastle upon Tyne, 1985.

12 Murray, *Families Divided* p. 10.

13 S. Turner, *The Underlying Causes of Poverty in Lesotho* (Maseru: Care, 2005), p. 9.

14 J. Crush, A. Jeeves and D. Yudelman, *South Africa's Labor Empire: A History of Black Migrancy to the Gold Mines* (Boulder and Cape Town: Westview and David Philip, 1991).

15 M. Molapo, "Job Stress, Health and Perceptions of Migrant Mineworkers" In J. Crush and W. James, eds., *Crossing Boundaries: Mine Migrancy in a Democratic South Africa* (Cape Town and Ottawa: Idasa and IDRC, 1995), pp. 88-99.

16 Van der Wiel, *Migratory Wage Labour* p. 22.

17 T. Sparreboom and P. Sparreboom-Burger, "Migrant Worker Remittances in Lesotho: A Review of the Deferred Pay Scheme" Working Paper No. 16, Enterprise and Cooperative Development Department, International Labour Office, Geneva, 1995.

18 M. Mueller, "Women and Men: Power and Powerlessness in Lesotho" *Signs* 3 (1) (1977): 154-66; Gordon, "Impact of Labour Migration on the Lives of Women in Lesotho."

19 P. Bonner, "'Desirable or Undesirable Basotho Women?' Liquor, Prostitution and the Migration of Basotho Women to the Rand, 1920-1945" In C. Walker, ed., *Women and Gender in Southern Africa to 1945* (Cape Town: David Philip and London: James Currey, 1990), pp. 221-50; E. Maloka, "*Khomo Lia Oela*: Canteens, Brothels and Labour Migrancy in Colonial Lesotho, 1900-40" *Journal of African History* 38 (1997): 101-22; and D. Coplan, "You Have Left Me Wandering About: Basotho Women and the Culture of Mobility" In D. Hodgson and S. McCurdy (Eds), *Wicked Women and the Reconfiguration of Gender in Africa* (Exeter, N.H.: Heinemann, 2001), pp. 188-211.

20 Murray, *Families Divided* p. 154.

21 These figures, from Statistics South Africa, refer to the number of recorded crossings, not the actual number of different individuals who crossed. Many Basotho cross into South Africa several times during the course of a year.

22 J. Gay, "Lesotho and South Africa: Time for a New Immigration Compact" In D. McDonald, ed., *On Borders: Perspectives on International Migration in Southern Africa* (New York and Cape Town: St Martin's Press and SAMP, 2000), pp. 25-45.

23   J. Crush and J. Gay, "Migration and Remittances in Lesotho: An Overview" Report for UN-INSTRAW, Santo Dominigo, Dominican Republic, 2008.

24   C. Tshitereke, "GEAR and Labour in Post-Apartheid South Africa: A Study of the Gold Mining Industry, 1987-2004" PhD Thesis, Queen's University, 2004.

25   G. Seidman, "Shafted: The Social Impact of Down-Scaling in the OFS Goldfields" In J. Crush and W. James, eds., *Crossing Boundaries: Mine Migrancy in a Democratic South Africa* (Cape Town and Ottawa: Idasa and IDRC, 1995), pp. 176-84; D. Coplan and T. Thoalane, "Motherless Households, Landless Farms: Employment Patterns Among Lesotho Migrants" In Crush and James, *Crossing Boundaries*.

26   C. Boehm, "The Social Life of Fields: Labour Markets and Agrarian Change in Lesotho" *Paideusis - Journal for Interdisciplinary and Cross-Cultural Studies* 3 (2003): 1-18.

27   Ibid.

28   The gold price increased from USD$260 per ounce in 2001 to USD$420 in 2004. In December 2009, the price reached over USD$1200 per ounce.

29   Interview with Head of Lesotho Office, National Union of Mineworkers (NUM), Maseru, January 2009.

30   Coplan and Thoalane, "Motherless Households, Landless Farms"; C. Sweetman, "The Miners Return: Changing Gender Relations in Lesotho's Ex-Migrants' Families" Gender Analysis in Development Series No. 9, University of East Anglia, 1995; N. Pule and K. Matlosa, *The Impact of Retrenched Returnees on Gender Relations in Rural Lesotho* (Addis Ababa: OSSREA, 2000); P. Magrath, "Changing Household Structures and Gender Relations in Lesotho" Report for CARE, Maseru, 2004.

31   Participant in Focus Group No 4, December 2008.

32   Participant in Focus Group No 2, December 2008.

33   Interview No 38, January 2009.

34   A. Salm, W. Grant, T. Green, J. Haycock and J. Raimondo, *Lesotho Garment Industry Sub-Sector Study for the Government of Lesotho* (Maseru, 2002), pp. 14-56.

35   S. Lall, "FDI, AGOA and Manufactured Exports by a Landlocked, Least Developed African Economy: Lesotho" *Journal of Development Studies* 41 (6) (2005): 998-1022.

36   M. Morris and L. Sedowski, "Report on Government Responses to New Post-MFA Realities in Lesotho" Report for the Institute for Global Dialogue, Johannesburg, 2006.

37   C. Baylies and C. Wright, "Female Labour in the Textile and Clothing Industry of Lesotho" *African Affairs* 92 (1993): 577-91; C. Wright, "Unemployment, Migration and Changing Gender Relations in Lesotho" PhD Thesis, University of Leeds, 1993.

38   S. Rosenberg, "South African and Global Apartheid: The Experience of Basotho Labor in the South African Gold Mines and Taiwanese-Owned

Textile Factories" *Safundi: The Journal of South African and American Studies* 8 (4) (2007): 459-72; G. Seidman, "Labouring Under an Illusion: Lesotho's "Sweat-Free" Label" *Third World Quarterly* 30 (3) (2009): 581-98.

39 C. Boehm, "Industrial Labour, Marital Strategy and Changing Livelihood Trajectories Among Young Women in Lesotho" In C. Christiansen, M. Utas and H. Vigh, eds., *Navigating Youth, Generating Adulthood: Social Becoming in an African Context* (Uppsala: Nordic Africa Institute, 2006), p. 156.

40 Ibid.

41 K. Dyer, "Gender Relations in the Home and the Workplace: A Case Study of the Gender Implications of Lesotho's Current Economic Development Strategy for the Clothing Industry" Institute of Southern African Studies (ISAS), National University of Lesotho, Roma, 2001; Boehm, "Industrial Labour, Marital Strategy and Changing Livelihood Trajectories", p. 5.

42 P. Tanga and T. Manyeli, "The Shifting Nature of the Living Conditions of the Peri-Urban Women: The Case of Ex-Employees of Textile Industries in Maseru, Lesotho" *International Journal of Emotional Psychology and Sport Ethics* 9 (2007): 28-43.

43 Salm et al, *Lesotho Garment Industry Sub-Sector Study.*

44 M. Bennet, "Lesotho's Export Textiles and Garment Industry" In H. Jauch and R. Traub-Merz (Eds), *The Future of the Textile and Clothing Industry in Sub-Saharan Africa* (Bonn:Friedrich-Ebert-Stiftung, 2006), pp.165-77.

45 Boehm, "Industrial Labour, Marital Strategy and Changing Livelihood Trajectories" p. 167.

46 Salm et al, *Lesotho Garment Industry Sub-Sector Study* p. 60.

47 J. Crush and B. Dodson, "Another Lost Decade: The Failures of South Africa's Post-Apartheid Migration Policy" *Tijdschrift voor Economishe en Sociale Geografie* 98 (4) (2007): 436-54.

48 D. Wason and D. Hall, "Poverty in Lesotho: 1993 to 2002: An Overview of Household Economic Status and Government Policy" Working Paper 40, IDPM/Chronic Poverty Research Centre (CPRC), University of Manchester, 2004, p. 2.

49 J. Crush, W. Pendleton and D. Tevera, "Degrees of Uncertainty: Students and the Brain Drain in Southern Africa" In R. Kishun, ed., *The Internationalisation of Higher Education in South Africa* (Durban: IEASA, 2006), pp. 123-44.

50 T. Green, "The Potential Brain Drain from Lesotho" In J. Crush, E. Campbell, T. Green, S. Nangulah and H. Simelane, *States of Vulnerability: The Future Brain Drain of Talent to South Africa*, SAMP Migration Policy Series No. 42, Cape Town, 2006, pp. 19-31.

51 J. Crush, B. Williams, M. Lurie and E. Gouws, "Migration and HIV/AIDS in South Africa" *Development Southern Africa* 22 (2005): 293-318; P. Banati, "Risk Amplification: HIV in Migrant Communities" *Development Southern Africa* 24 (1) (2007): 205-23; M. Coffee, M. Lurie and G. Garnett, "Modelling the Impact of Migration on the HIV Epidemic in South Africa" *AIDS* 21(3) (2007): 343-50.

52 N. Romero-Daza and D. Himmelgreen, "More Than Money for Your Labor. Migration and the Political Economy of AIDS in Lesotho" In M. Singer, ed., *The Political Economy of AIDS* (Amityville, NY: Baywood Press, 1998), pp. 185-204.

53 D. Wilson, *Lesotho and Swaziland:.HIV/AIDS Risk Assessments at Cross Border and Migrant Sites in Southern Africa* (Arlington: Family Health International, 2001), p. 11.

54 Family Health International (FHI), Lesotho Ministry of Health, LAPCA, Sechaba Consultants and USAID (2002), *HIV/AIDS Behavioral Surveillance Survey: Lesotho* Maseru, 2002.

55 Ibid.; T. Makatjane, "Pre-Marital Sex and Childbearing in Lesotho" *African Population Studies* 17 (2) (2002): 99-112.

56 Wilson, HIV/AIDS Risk Assessments at Cross Border and Migrant Sites p. 5; N. Waterman, "Commercial Sex Workers: Adult Education and Pathways Out of Poverty" In J. Preece, ed., *Adult Education and Poverty Reduction: A Global Priority* (Gaborone: University of Botswana, 2004), pp. 395-400.

57 Wilson, *HIV/AIDS Risk Assessments at Cross Border and Migrant Sites*, p. 2.

58 C. Campbell, "Migrancy, Masculine Identities and AIDS: The Psychosocial Context of HIV Transmission on the South African Gold Mines" *Social Science & Medicine* 45 (2) (1997): 273-81; D. Meekers, "Going Underground and Going After Women: Trends in Sexual Risk Behaviour Among Gold Miners in South Africa" *International Journal of STD and AIDS* 11 (2000): 21-6.

59 Wilson, *HIV/AIDS Risk Assessments at Cross Border and Migrant Sites*, p. 5.

60 I. Kimane, M. Moteetee and T. Green, "'How Can You Tell the Sun Not to Shine?' Knowledge, Attitudes and Practices of Basotho Migrants (Miners and Farm Workers) in Relation to HIV/AIDS and Sexually Transmitted Infections" Report for Ministry of Employment and Labour, Maseru, 2004.

61 Participant in Focus Group No 2.

62 Government of Lesotho, *Lesotho Demographic and Health Survey* (Maseru: Ministry of Health and Social Welfare & Bureau of Statistics, 2005).

63 S. Clark, M. Collinson, K. Kahn, K., Drullinger and S. Tollman, "Returning Home to Die: Circular Labour Migration and Mortality in South Africa" *Scandinavian Journal of Public Health* 35 (2007): 35-44.

64 L. Young and N. Ansell, "Fluid Households, Complex Families: The Impacts of Children's Migration as a Response to HIV/AIDS in Southern Africa" *Professional Geographer* 55 (4) (2003): 464–76; N. Ansel and L. van Blerk, *HIV/AIDS and Children's Migration in Southern Africa*, SAMP Migration Policy Series No. 33, Cape Town, 2004; N. Ansell and L. van Blerk, "Children's Migration as a Household/Family Strategy: Coping with AIDS in Malawi and Lesotho" *Journal of Southern African Studies* 30 (3) (2004): 673-90; L. van Blerk and N. Ansell, "Children's Experiences of Migration: Moving in the Wake of AIDS in Southern Africa" *Environment and Planning D: Society and Space* 24 (3) (2006): 449-71.

65   Turner, *Underlying Causes of Poverty in Lesotho*.
66   P. Magrath, "Changing Household Structures and Gender Relations in Lesotho" Report for CARE, Maseru, 2004, p. 18.
67   Crush and James, *Crossing Boundaries*; Government of South Africa, *Report of the Leon Commission of Inquiry into Safety and Health in the Mining Industry*, 2 Volumes (Pretoria), 1995; J. Crush, T. Ulicki, T. Tseane and E. Jansen Van Vuuren, "Undermining Labour: The Social Impact of Sub-Contracting on the South African Gold Mines" *Journal of Southern African Studies* 27(1999): 5-31; M. Hermanus and C. Marx, "The South African Experience in Mine Safety" *Journal of Mines, Metals and Fuels* 49 (2001): 92-6.
68   Crush et al, "Undermining Labour"; L. Sikakane, "Subcontracting in Gold Mining: Western Deep Level Mine, Carletonville" M.A. Thesis, University of Johannesburg, 2003.
69   M. Dibetle, "Dying for Gold" *Mail & Guardian* 15 June 2009.
70   D. Johnston, "Migration and Poverty in Lesotho: A Case Study of Female Farm Labourers" PhD Thesis, University of London, 1997; T. Ulicki and J. Crush, "Gender, Farmwork, and Women's Migration from Lesotho to the New South Africa" *Canadian Journal of African Studies* 34 (1) (2000): 64-79; D. Johnston, "Who Needs Immigrant Farm Workers? A South African Case Study" *Journal of Agrarian Change* 7(4) (2007): 494-525; T. Ulicki and J. Crush, "Poverty, Gender and Migrancy: Lesotho's Migrant Farmworkers" *Development Southern Africa* 24 (1) (2007): 155-72.
71   Ulicki and Crush, "Gender, Farmwork, and Women's Migration from Lesotho"; Ulicki and Crush, "Poverty, Gender and Migrancy."
72   N. Dinat and S. Peberdy, "Worlds of Work, Health and Migration: Domestic Workers in Johannesburg" *Development Southern Africa* 24(1) (2007): 187-204.
73   Interview with Director: Immigration, Lesotho, January 2009.
74   Interview with Director of Consular Services: Department of Foreign Affairs, January 2009.
75   Participant in Focus Group 2.
76   Sparreboom and Sparreboom-Burger, "Migrant Worker Remittances in Lesotho."
77   F. Hassan, *Lesotho: Development in a Challenging Environment* (Abidjan and Washington: African Development Bank and World Bank, 2002); M. Makoae, "Knowledge Review and Gap Analysis: Hunger and Vulnerability in Lesotho" Regional Hunger and Vulnerability Programme; UNDP-Lesotho, 2006; Government of Lesotho, *Lesotho National Human Development Report 2006* (Morija: Morija Printing Works, 2007).
78   T. Green, "Migration and Poverty in Lesotho" Report for Southern African Migration Project, Maseru, 2006.
79   Genesis Analytics, "Access to Financial Services in Lesotho" FinMark Trust Research Paper No. 2, Johannesburg, 2003, p. 22.
80   Genesis Analytics, "African Families, African Money: Bridging the Money Transfer Divide" Report for FinMark Trust, Johannesburg, 2003, p. vi.

81 Ibid., p. ix.
82 Genesis Analytics, "Supporting Remittances in Southern Africa" p. 12.
83 Genesis Analytics, "Facilitating Southern African Remittance Networks" Paper for the Commonwealth Secretariat Workshop on Foreign Remittances and Development in the SADC Region, Maseru, 2006, p. 6.
84 Interview No 33, January 2009
85 Interview No 25, January 2009.
86 Participant in Focus Group 2.
87 Table 30 shows the reported average amount of the previous month's expenditure in various categories, using median rather than mean values to provide a more accurate reflection of average expenditure levels, as this reduces the influence of one or two respondent households with high expenditure. Note too that the values in Table 43 are only for those households reporting the particular expenditure (i.e. excluding the 'zero-expenditure' households in each category), and also represent expenditure in a particular single month rather than averaged over a year.
88 Participant in Focus Group 3, December 2008.
89 Participant in Focus Group 4.
90 Interview No 35, January 2009.
91 Participant in Focus Group 2.
92 Interview No 33, January 2009.
93 Sechaba Consultants, *Poverty in Lesotho: A Mapping Exercise* (Maseru, 1991); Sechaba Consultants, *Poverty in Lesotho 1994: A Mapping Exercise* (Maseru, 1994); Sechaba Consultants, *Lesotho's Long Journey: Hard Choices at the Crossroads* (Maseru, 1995); Sechaba Consultants, *Poverty and Livelihoods in Lesotho 2000: More Than a Mapping Exercise* (Maseru, 2000); World Bank, *Lesotho Poverty Assessment*, World Bank Sector Report No. 13171, Washington, 1995; J. May, B. Roberts, G. Moqasa and I. Woolard, "Poverty and Inequality in Lesotho" CSDS Working Paper No 36, University of Natal, Durban, 2002; D. Omole, "Poverty in Lesotho: A Case Study and Policy Options" Department of Economics, National University of Lesotho, 2003.
94 May et al, "Poverty and Inequality in Lesotho."
95 Poverty Line of M124 per person per month in 2001 prices; May et al, "Poverty and Inequality in Lesotho" p. 4.
96 Wason and Hall, "Poverty in Lesotho: 1993 to 2002"; D. Gill-Wason, "Evolving Livelihood Strategies of Rural Basotho: 1993 to 2002" Report for CARE Lesotho-South Africa, Maseru, 2004.
97 Wason and Hall, "Poverty in Lesotho: 1993 to 2002" p. 23.
98 Green, "Migration and Poverty in Lesotho."
99 The LPI is based on answers to questions about how often the people in the household have had sufficient basic items in the previous year: food, water, medicine, cooking fuel and cash income. Answers are collected in five categories: never, just once or twice, several times, many times, always.

100 Forum for Food Security, "Maize, Mines or Manufacturing? Options for Reducing Hunger in Lesotho" Country Food Security Options Paper No 1, Forum for Food Security in Southern Africa, Maseru, 2002, p. 11; M. Mphale, E., Rwambali and Sechaba Consultants, "Lesotho Food Security Issues Paper" Forum for Food Security in Southern Africa, Maseru, 2003.

101 Turner, *Underlying Causes of Poverty in Lesotho* p. 11.

102 Interview No 45, December 2008.

103 Interview No 41, December 2008.

104 Interview No 50, December 2008.

105 Interview No. 51, January 2009.

106 Participant in Focus Group 2.

107 Ibid.

108 Participant in Focus Group 3.

109 Ibid.

110 Participant in Focus Group 2.

111 Participant in Focus Group 1, December 2008.

112 Participant in Focus Group 2.

113 Participant in Focus Group 3.

114 Participant in Focus Group 1.

115 Participant in Focus Group 3.

116 Participant in Focus Group 1.

117 Sechaba Consultants, *The Border Within: The Future of the Lesotho-South African International Boundary*. SAMP Migration Policy Series No. 26, Cape Town, 2002.

118 H. De Haas, "Mobility and Human Development" Human Development Research Paper No 1/2009, UNDP, New York, p. 1.

119 Gay, "Lesotho and South Africa: Time for a New Immigration Compact."

120 The International Convention on the Protection of the Rights of All Migrant Workers and Members of their Families.

121 Gay, "Lesotho and South Africa: Time for a New Immigration Compact."

122 V. Williams, J. Crush and P. Nicholson, "The UN Convention on the Rights of Migrant Workers: The South African Non-Debate" SAMP Migration Policy Brief No. 21, Cape Town, 2006.

123 Sechaba Consultants, *The Border Within*.

MIGRATION POLICY SERIES

1. *Covert Operations: Clandestine Migration, Temporary Work and Immigration Policy in South Africa* (1997) ISBN 1-874864-51-9
2. *Riding the Tiger: Lesotho Miners and Permanent Residence in South Africa* (1997) ISBN 1-874864-52-7
3. *International Migration, Immigrant Entrepreneurs and South Africa's Small Enterprise Economy* (1997) ISBN 1-874864-62-4
4. *Silenced by Nation Building: African Immigrants and Language Policy in the New South Africa* (1998) ISBN 1-874864-64-0
5. *Left Out in the Cold? Housing and Immigration in the New South Africa* (1998) ISBN 1-874864-68-3
6. *Trading Places: Cross-Border Traders and the South African Informal Sector* (1998) ISBN 1-874864-71-3
7. *Challenging Xenophobia: Myth and Realities about Cross-Border Migration in Southern Africa* (1998) ISBN 1-874864-70-5
8. *Sons of Mozambique: Mozambican Miners and Post-Apartheid South Africa* (1998) ISBN 1-874864-78-0
9. *Women on the Move: Gender and Cross-Border Migration to South Africa* (1998) ISBN 1-874864-82-9.
10. *Namibians on South Africa: Attitudes Towards Cross-Border Migration and Immigration Policy* (1998) ISBN 1-874864-84-5.
11. *Building Skills: Cross-Border Migrants and the South African Construction Industry* (1999) ISBN 1-874864-84-5
12. *Immigration & Education: International Students at South African Universities and Technikons* (1999) ISBN 1-874864-89-6
13. *The Lives and Times of African Immigrants in Post-Apartheid South Africa* (1999) ISBN 1-874864-91-8
14. *Still Waiting for the Barbarians: South African Attitudes to Immigrants and Immigration* (1999) ISBN 1-874864-91-8
15. *Undermining Labour: Migrancy and Sub-contracting in the South African Gold Mining Industry* (1999) ISBN 1-874864-91-8
16. *Borderline Farming: Foreign Migrants in South African Commercial Agriculture* (2000) ISBN 1-874864-97-7
17. *Writing Xenophobia: Immigration and the Press in Post-Apartheid South Africa* (2000) ISBN 1-919798-01-3
18. *Losing Our Minds: Skills Migration and the South African Brain Drain* (2000) ISBN 1-919798-03-x
19. *Botswana: Migration Perspectives and Prospects* (2000) ISBN 1-919798-04-8
20. *The Brain Gain: Skilled Migrants and Immigration Policy in Post-Apartheid South Africa* (2000) ISBN 1-919798-14-5
21. *Cross-Border Raiding and Community Conflict in the Lesotho-South African Border Zone* (2001) ISBN 1-919798-16-1

22. *Immigration, Xenophobia and Human Rights in South Africa* (2001) ISBN 1-919798-30-7
23. *Gender and the Brain Drain from South Africa* (2001) ISBN 1-919798-35-8
24. *Spaces of Vulnerability: Migration and HIV/AIDS in South Africa* (2002) ISBN 1-919798-38-2
25. *Zimbabweans Who Move: Perspectives on International Migration in Zimbabwe* (2002) ISBN 1-919798-40-4
26. *The Border Within: The Future of the Lesotho-South African International Boundary* (2002) ISBN 1-919798-41-2
27. *Mobile Namibia: Migration Trends and Attitudes* (2002) ISBN 1-919798-44-7
28. *Changing Attitudes to Immigration and Refugee Policy in Botswana* (2003) ISBN 1-919798-47-1
29. *The New Brain Drain from Zimbabwe* (2003) ISBN 1-919798-48-X
30. *Regionalizing Xenophobia? Citizen Attitudes to Immigration and Refugee Policy in Southern Africa* (2004) ISBN 1-919798-53-6
31. *Migration, Sexuality and HIV/AIDS in Rural South Africa* (2004) ISBN 1-919798-63-3
32. *Swaziland Moves: Perceptions and Patterns of Modern Migration* (2004) ISBN 1-919798-67-6
33. *HIV/AIDS and Children's Migration in Southern Africa* (2004) ISBN 1-919798-70-6
34. *Medical Leave: The Exodus of Health Professionals from Zimbabwe* (2005) ISBN 1-919798-74-9
35. *Degrees of Uncertainty: Students and the Brain Drain in Southern Africa* (2005) ISBN 1-919798-84-6
36. *Restless Minds: South African Students and the Brain Drain* (2005) ISBN 1-919798-82-X
37. *Understanding Press Coverage of Cross-Border Migration in Southern Africa since 2000* (2005) ISBN 1-919798-91-9
38. *Northern Gateway: Cross-Border Migration Between Namibia and Angola* (2005) ISBN 1-919798-92-7
39. *Early Departures: The Emigration Potential of Zimbabwean Students* (2005) ISBN 1-919798-99-4
40. *Migration and Domestic Workers: Worlds of Work, Health and Mobility in Johannesburg* (2005) ISBN 1-920118-02-0
41. *The Quality of Migration Services Delivery in South Africa* (2005) ISBN 1-920118-03-9
42. *States of Vulnerability: The Future Brain Drain of Talent to South Africa* (2006) ISBN 1-920118-07-1
43. *Migration and Development in Mozambique: Poverty, Inequality and Survival* (2006) ISBN 1-920118-10-1
44. *Migration, Remittances and Development in Southern Africa* (2006) ISBN 1-920118-15-2

45. *Medical Recruiting: The Case of South African Health Care Professionals* (2007) ISBN 1-920118-47-0
46. *Voices From the Margins: Migrant Women's Experiences in Southern Africa* (2007) ISBN 1-920118-50-0
47. *The Haemorrhage of Health Professionals From South Africa: Medical Opinions* (2007) ISBN 978-1-920118-63-1
48. *The Quality of Immigration and Citizenship Services in Namibia* (2008) ISBN 978-1-920118-67-9
49. *Gender, Migration and Remittances in Southern Africa* (2008) ISBN 978-1-920118-70-9
50. *The Perfect Storm: The Realities of Xenophobia in Contemporary South Africa* (2008) ISBN 978-1-920118-71-6
51. *Migrant Remittances and Household Survival in Zimbabwe* (2009) ISBN 978-1-920118-92-1 2009